CAMPAIGN 290

ATLANTA 1864

Sherman marches South

JAMES DONNELL

ILLUSTRATED BY STEVE NOON
Series editor Marcus Cowper

First published in Great Britain in 2016 by Osprey Publishing,
PO Box 883, Oxford, OX1 9PL, UK
PO Box 3985, New York, NY 10185-3985, USA
E-mail: info@ospreypublishing.com

A CIP catalog record for this book is available from the British Library.

ISBN: 978 1 4728 1153 0
PDF e-book ISBN: 978 1 4728 1154 7
e-Pub ISBN: 978 1 4728 1155 4

Editorial by Ilios Publishing Ltd, Oxford, UK (www.iliospublishing.com)
Index by Alan Rutter
Typeset in Myriad Pro and Sabon
Maps by Bounford.com
3D bird's-eye views by The Black Spot
Battlescene illustrations by Steve Noon
Originated by PDQ Media, Bungay, UK
Printed in China through Worldprint Ltd.

16 17 18 19 20   10 9 8 7 6 5 4 3 2 1

ACKNOWLEDGEMENT

This book simply would not have been possible without the innumerable
contributions of my wife, Amelia, and the support of my entire family.
Thank you!

ARTIST'S NOTE

Readers may care to note that the original paintings from which the color
plates in this book were prepared are available for private sale. The
Publishers retain all reproduction copyright whatsoever. All enquiries
should be addressed to:

www.steve-noon.co.uk

The Publishers regret that they can enter into no correspondence upon this
matter.

THE WOODLAND TRUST

Osprey Publishing are supporting the Woodland Trust, the UK's leading
woodland conservation charity, by funding the dedication of trees.

TITLE PAGE:
The battle of Chickamauga elevated Union General
George Thomas to hero status while effectively ending
the once-promising career of William Rosecrans. (LOC)

Key to military symbols

xxxxx Army Group	xxxx Army	xxx Corps	xx Division	x Brigade	III Regiment	II Battalion
I Company/Battery	••• Platoon	•• Section	• Squad	Infantry	Artillery	Cavalry
Airborne	Unit HQ	Air defense	Air Force	Air mobile	Air transportable	Amphibious
Antitank	Armor	Air aviation	Bridging	Engineer	Headquarters	Maintenance
Medical	Missile	Mountain	Navy	Nuclear, biological, chemical	Ordnance	Parachute
Reconnaissance	Signal	Supply	Transport movement	Rocket artillery	Air defense artillery	

Key to unit identification

Unit identifier | Parent unit
Commander
(+) with added elements
(–) less elements

CONTENTS

THE STRATEGIC SITUATION

Lieutenant-General Ulysses S. Grant. "Well, I wish some of you would tell me the brand of whiskey that Grant drinks. I would like to send a barrel of it to my other generals." Abraham Lincoln, after the fall of Vicksburg. (Photograph from the Library of Congress (LOC) Prints and Photographs Division)

The summer of 1864 saw a decided shift in the Union's strategic application of military power. For three years, President Abraham Lincoln had struggled to find commanders who would not only take the fight to the enemy, but would also avoid being continually outmaneuvered by their Confederate counterparts. Ulysses S. Grant had his detractors, but Lincoln was not one of them. "I like him, he fights," the President explained to those who would have preferred someone else to lead a Federal Army that had an indisputable advantage in manpower and logistics over its opponent. Grant had won a series of dramatic victories, beginning with Forts Henry and Donelson in 1862 and culminating with the battles of Lookout Mountain and Missionary Ridge, which had forced a Confederate withdrawal from Chattanooga, Tennessee, into northwest Georgia in November 1863. Now Grant was needed in the east because, despite those victories, the outcome of the war was still very much in question.

The US Presidential Election of 1864 promised to be a referendum on Lincoln's conduct of the war. Both sides were weary of the fighting. Combined combat deaths were rapidly approaching half a million men. The Democratic platform supported ending the war immediately. European nations watched and waited for a sign that the Confederacy would survive. Lincoln needed a dramatic victory. Gettysburg had ended the most recent attempt at an invasion of the North, but Lee's Army survived, as did General Joseph E. Johnston's Army of Tennessee, now solidly entrenched along Rocky Face Ridge, less than 30 miles south of Chattanooga.

President Jefferson Davis had reluctantly assigned Johnston to his current command after the fall of Chattanooga, more as a result of popular sentiment than from any belief in his capabilities. The two had been at odds since the war began over Johnston's ranking within the hierarchy of Confederate generals, as well as his failure to keep Davis as fully informed of his intentions as the latter thought necessary. Davis was sensitive about his knowledge of military affairs and not one to overlook a perceived slight, and Johnston's career waxed and waned along with the fate of the Confederacy, demonstrating that the South was not without its own leadership issues.

Southerners still believed that one Confederate soldier equaled ten Union men. Lee would continue to demonstrate his genius in the Overland Campaign in a series of titanic battles against Grant and Major-General George Meade, the newest commander of the Army of the Potomac. But he had indeed lost his "right arm" when the "Mighty Stonewall" died from wounds received at the hands of his own men at Chancellorsville, and Lee knew it would take more than brilliance to overcome the deficiencies the South faced.

Southern leadership continued to express optimism in its assessment of the overall situation facing it in the winter of 1863–64, vociferously exclaiming that ultimate victory was within its grasp. In a letter of instruction to Johnston in December 1863, Confederate Secretary of War James A. Seddon stated, "It is apprehended that the army may have been, by recent events, somewhat disheartened, and deprived of ordnance and material. Your presence, it is hoped, will do much to reestablish hope and inspire confidence." There was no question about the direction Johnston's planning should take. "As soon as the condition of your forces will allow, it is hoped you will be able to resume the offensive."

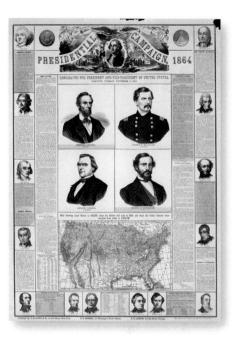

Campaign poster for the Presidential Election of 1864. The Democrats advocated ending the war and letting the South go its own way. The Republicans warned voters, "Don't change horses in midstream." (LOC)

Johnston was offended by the tone of the letter, deeming it an affront to someone with his military experience. After conducting a thorough assessment of his new command, he responded accordingly. "This army is now far from being in condition to 'resume the offensive.' It is deficient in numbers, arms, subsistence stores, and field transportation." Over the next seven months, he would work diligently to improve his army's situation while continuing to fend off criticism from Richmond.

The battles in the western theater had always been as dramatic and bloody as anything occurring in the east. In April 1862, Grant's Army of the Tennessee had narrowly avoided defeat at Shiloh, also known as Pittsburg Landing. Grant, and his senior division commander, William Tecumseh Sherman, seriously underestimated the rebel army's intentions, with Grant admitting later that he had "scarcely the faintest idea of an attack." His counterattack on the second day turned the tide, forcing the Confederates to abandon the field. In the clash, the South lost one of its most capable generals, Albert Sydney Johnston.

In the summer of 1863, while Grant was working to force the surrender of Vicksburg, the last Confederate bastion on the Mississippi, Major-General William Rosecrans, commander of the Union Army of the Cumberland, was attempting to outmaneuver the Confederate Army of Tennessee, then under General Braxton Bragg. Rosecrans' actions during the Tullahoma Campaign pushed Bragg out of middle Tennessee and threatened the Confederate hold on Chattanooga. Bragg was eventually forced to abandon the city, but Rosecrans' offensive, and, effectively, his once-bright military career came to an ignominious end at the battle of Chickamauga in September 1863.

During the battle, one-third of the Union Army, along with Rosecrans himself, was driven from the field. Only the stubbornness of Major-General George Thomas, who earned the sobriquet "The Rock of Chickamauga" for his refusal to yield to repeated rebel assaults, saved the Union Army from complete annihilation. The Confederates claimed victory while Rosecrans

and the remnants of his shattered command found themselves besieged in Chattanooga. Bragg's army held the high ground south and east of the city, occupying the critical points of Lookout Mountain and Missionary Ridge.

In October, Lincoln appointed Grant to command the newly formed Division of the Mississippi, with responsibility for all Union forces in the western theater. When Grant learned of Rosecrans' inability to break the siege, he replaced him with Thomas, then he rode to Chattanooga to take charge of the situation. Lincoln had also sent Major-General Joseph Hooker with two divisions of the Army of the Potomac to reinforce Thomas. Grant used Hooker's troops to establish a supply route known as the "Cracker Line," effectively ending the siege.

Grant was not about to stop there. In mid-November, he brought the Army of the Tennessee, now under Sherman, from Vicksburg, Mississippi. On the afternoon of November 23, Thomas's Army of the Cumberland maneuvered east of the city to seize a section of high ground known as Orchard Knob, while elements of Sherman's army launched a surprise attack on Bragg's right flank on Missionary Ridge. The next morning, Hooker's divisions scaled the "inaccessible heights of Lookout Mountain," in an engagement known as the "Battle above the Clouds," forcing Bragg to concentrate his forces east of Chattanooga. There, on November 25, the battle of Missionary Ridge broke the Confederate line. Bragg gave up southern Tennessee and retreated to Dalton, Georgia.

Bragg resigned as commander of the Army of Tennessee on December 1, and was temporarily replaced by Lieutenant-General William J. Hardee. On December 27, Johnston took over the command while Bragg went to Richmond to serve as President Jefferson Davis's chief military adviser. Davis and Bragg had been friends since the Mexican War, a situation that did nothing to ease the strained relationship between Davis and Johnston.

The Battle above the Clouds. The Confederates held the high ground south of Chattanooga until Hooker's XII Corps climbed the unassailable heights of Lookout Mountain, November 24, 1863. (LOC)

At the time, the debate was raging over the best approach to take to ensure the survival of the Confederacy. Southern strategy had evolved since 1861. In his initial address to the Confederate Congress, President Davis stated, "We ask no conquest, no aggrandizement, no concern of any kind from the States, all we ask is to be left alone." But a completely defensive posture soon became "offensive-defensive" as opportunity presented itself on the battlefield. This remained the case in 1864, even when the reality of the discrepancy in resources between the two warring sides became increasingly obvious. Johnston, and other senior officers, felt that the South's best chance lay in a drawn-out war of attrition designed to defeat the will of the enemy to continue fighting. Davis, on the other hand, believed that victory could come only through direct combat, and pressed Johnston to take up the offensive, if for no other reason than to take pressure off Lee in Virginia.

Johnston tried to convince his superiors that it would work to their great advantage to allow Union troops to batter themselves against the Confederate entrenchments: "I therefore thought it our policy to stand on the defensive, to spare the blood of our soldiers by fighting under cover habitually, and to attack only when bad position or division of the enemy's forces might give us advantages counterbalancing that of superior numbers." Then, when the balance of power shifted in his favor, as it eventually must, Johnston would push the enemy not only out of Georgia, but out of Tennessee as well.

In the spring of 1864, an event rivaling in importance the appointment of Robert E. Lee as commander of the Army of Northern Virginia occurred in the Union Army. In March, Grant was promoted to lieutenant-general and named supreme commander of all Union armies. While the rallying cry for the Federal Army in the early days of the war had been "On to Richmond," Grant believed differently. "The art of war is simple enough. Find out where your enemy is. Get at him as soon as you can. Strike him as hard as you can, and keep moving on." Strategic objectives would henceforth be driven more by the location of the enemy's army than by the location of his capital.

"My general plan now was to concentrate all the force possible against the Confederate armies in the field," Grant wrote. The North had envisioned their "Anaconda Plan" in 1861, to strangle the South into submission, but they had allowed the various military commanders to operate independently. "I determined to stop this," Grant stated. "I arranged for a simultaneous movement all along the line."

While Meade, with Grant by his side, went after Lee in Virginia, Sherman, the newly appointed commander of the Division of the Mississippi, would lead his three subordinate armies against Johnston. Simultaneously, Major-General Benjamin Butler would take the Army of the James from Fort Monroe, on the Virginia Peninsula, towards Richmond and Petersburg, on Lee's flank, and Major-General Franz Sigel would advance up the Shenandoah Valley from Harper's Ferry, Virginia. Finally, Major-General Nathaniel Banks, commanding the Department of the Gulf at New Orleans, Louisiana, would advance towards Mobile. The beginning of May was set as the start of the campaign.

General Robert E. Lee. Despite impressive victories at the Wilderness and Cold Harbor, in May and June 1864, Lee simply could not replace the 32,000 Confederate casualties, while Grant's loss of 50,000 was barely a bump in the road. (LOC)

Atlanta before the campaign. The future capital of Georgia was the center of the major manufacturing area in the South, second only to Richmond in importance to the Confederacy. (LOC)

Grant's orders to Sherman were, "to move against Johnston's army, to break it up, and to get into the interior of the enemy's country as far as you can, inflicting all the damage you can against their war resources." Sherman determined to use his much larger Federal army to crush Johnston as close to the Federal supply base at Chattanooga as possible. With Johnston and his army gone, Atlanta would quickly follow.

Atlanta's factories made munitions, guns, saddles, clothing, and other basic supplies, and Georgia was the breadbasket for the South's two remaining grand armies. Lee relied on Georgia for not only his subsistence, but also for possible reinforcements from Johnston's army. More importantly, Atlanta was the hub for four major rail lines. The Georgia Railroad went through Augusta and connected with Charleston, Wilmington, and Norfolk; the Macon & Western ran to Savannah; and the Atlanta & West Point provided a link to Alabama, including the all-important port of Mobile. Finally, the Western & Atlantic connected Atlanta with Chattanooga, and it was that line that had the attention of both Sherman and Johnston.

"The Atlanta campaign would simply not have been possible without this road," Sherman wrote, "that all our battles were fought for its possession, and that the Western and Atlantic Railroad of Georgia should be the pride of every true American by reason of its existence the Union was saved." In order to keep his army supplied, Sherman determined that he would need 130 railroad cars, each carrying 10 tons of supply, arriving at Chattanooga each day. Johnston, also depending on the Western & Atlantic for supplies, understood Sherman's position. "I was confident, too," he wrote, "that the Administration would see the expediency of employing [Major-General Nathan Bedford] Forrest, and his cavalry to break the enemy's railroad communications, by which he could have been defeated."

Johnston's position at Dalton had been selected more by chance than by

The Western & Atlantic Railroad. Begun in 1836, the rail line runs for 138 miles from Chattanooga to the former zero-milepost town of Terminus, renamed Atlanta in 1845. (Author's collection)

any brilliant stroke of military planning. After the Confederate Army was routed from Missionary Ridge, Bragg halted 30 miles south of Chattanooga and fortified a craggy 1,500-foot mountain called Rocky Face Ridge, awaiting the next Federal assault. Major-General Patrick Cleburne's division mounted a fierce rearguard stand at Ringgold, convincing the Federals to turn back, and the Army of Tennessee camped in Dalton for the winter. "The position at Dalton had little to recommend it as a defensive one,"

Johnston wrote. "It had neither intrinsic strength nor strategic value." He would have preferred to pull back to the vicinity of Calhoun, "to free our left flank from exposure," a situation which would eventually prove out, "but for the earnestness with which the President and Secretary of War, in their letters of instructions, wrote of early assumption of offensive operations."

Johnston did his best to prepare his army for the ensuing campaign: drilling his men, building up supplies, improving his defenses, and acquiring reinforcements. He attempted to reassure Davis and Bragg that his current defensive state was only temporary. In late March he wrote, "I expressly accept *taking the offensive*. Only differ with you as to the details." He continued, "I assume the enemy will be prepared *to advance before we are*, and will make it to our advantage." His assumption was absolutely correct.

Sherman had three grand armies at his disposal with a numerical superiority over Johnston approaching 2:1. The largest, Thomas's Army of the Cumberland, numbered 60,773 in three infantry corps and one cavalry corps. The smaller Army of the Tennessee, Sherman's former command, was now under the direction of Major-General James B. McPherson, and counted three corps totaling 24,465 men. The Army of the Ohio, under Major-General John M. Schofield, consisted of one corps and one cavalry division totaling 13,559. Supporting the troops were 254 cannon.

At the outset, Johnston reported nearly 42,856 officers and men present for duty with 154 cannon. Within days of the start of the campaign, he would be reinforced by Lieutenant-General Leonidas Polk's 15,000-man Army of Mississippi. That addition would give him a larger force than Lee had to battle Grant in Virginia.

"By the 27th of April spring had so far advanced as to justify me in fixing a day for the great move." Grant wrote. Along with his instructions to Meade, Butler, and Sigel, "Sherman was directed to get his forces up ready to advance on the 5th." Major-General Montgomery Meigs, Quartermaster-General of the Union Army, reported to Sherman, "five months supplies of all kinds are at Nashville. The great work on this side is nearly all done." Brigadier-General J. L. Donaldson, the Chief Quartermaster for the Department of the Cumberland, stated, "Sherman will move if he has to eat his mules."

On May 1, Sherman telegraphed Grant, "Schofield is now at Charleston, and will move to Cleveland. Thomas will concentrate at Ringgold, and McPherson's troops are all in motion toward Chattanooga, and by May 5 I will group them at Rossville and Gordon's Mills." The next day, Johnston telegraphed Bragg, "Our Scouts report re-enforcements to the enemy continually arriving, and preparations to advance, including repair of railroad from Cleveland to Red Clay." Bragg replied that Johnston "was deceived, probably by *mere demonstrations*, made for the purpose."

When the reality of Sherman's advance manifested itself, a southern newspaper warned, "Neither life nor virtue is sacred from these northern barbarians; the old and infirm perish by their bloody hands, while lovely women – our wives and daughters – are reserved for a fate even worse than death. Strike, men of the south and exterminate such polluted wretches, such living demons!"

Sherman's telegraph to Grant continued, "The first move will be: Thomas, Tunnel Hill; Schofield, Catoosa Springs, and McPherson, Villanow. Next move will be battle." The Atlanta campaign had begun.

General Braxton Bragg was considered intelligent, energetic, and a good planner, but seemed to annoy everyone who had to work with or for him. (LOC)

Strategic Overview

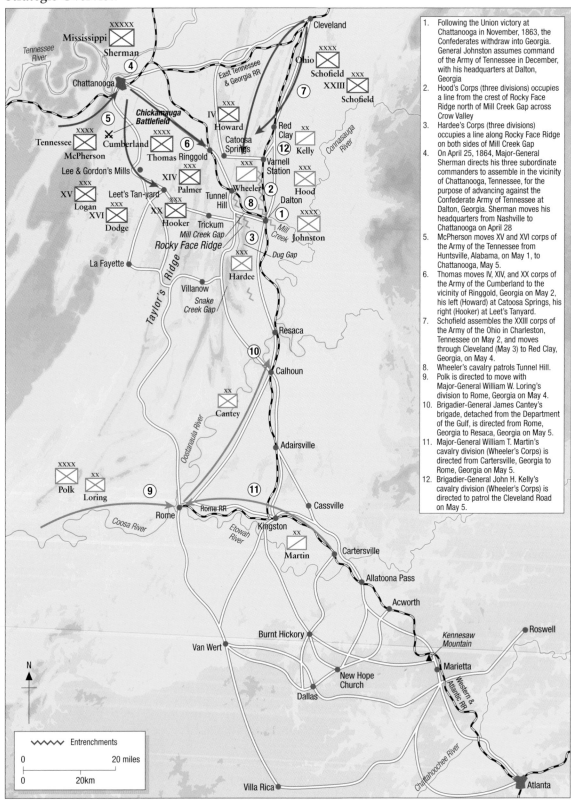

1. Following the Union victory at Chattanooga in November, 1863, the Confederates withdraw into Georgia. General Johnston assumes command of the Army of Tennessee in December, with his headquarters at Dalton, Georgia
2. Hood's Corps (three divisions) occupies a line from the crest of Rocky Face Ridge north of Mill Creek Gap across Crow Valley
3. Hardee's Corps (three divisions) occupies a line along Rocky Face Ridge on both sides of Mill Creek Gap
4. On April 25, 1864, Major-General Sherman directs his three subordinate commanders to assemble in the vicinity of Chattanooga, Tennessee, for the purpose of advancing against the Confederate Army of Tennessee at Dalton, Georgia. Sherman moves his headquarters from Nashville to Chattanooga on April 28
5. McPherson moves XV and XVI corps of the Army of the Tennessee from Huntsville, Alabama, on May 1, to Chattanooga, May 5.
6. Thomas moves IV, XIV, and XX corps of the Army of the Cumberland to the vicinity of Ringgold, Georgia on May 2, his left (Howard) at Catoosa Springs, his right (Hooker) at Leet's Tanyard.
7. Schofield assembles the XXIII corps of the Army of the Ohio in Charleston, Tennessee on May 2, and moves through Cleveland (May 3) to Red Clay, Georgia, on May 4.
8. Wheeler's cavalry patrols Tunnel Hill.
9. Polk is directed to move with Major-General William W. Loring's division to Rome, Georgia on May 4.
10. Brigadier-General James Cantey's brigade, detached from the Department of the Gulf, is directed from Rome, Georgia to Resaca, Georgia on May 5.
11. Major-General William T. Martin's cavalry division (Wheeler's Corps) is directed from Cartersville, Georgia to Rome, Georgia on May 5.
12. Brigadier-General John H. Kelly's cavalry division (Wheeler's Corps) is directed to patrol the Cleveland Road on May 5.

CHRONOLOGY

April 24	Federal scouts probe Rebel strength south of Ringgold, Georgia
27	Troop movement begins for Federal Army of the Tennessee. Union scouts probe enemy strength at Tunnel Hill
May 1–6	Union troops in all departments begin to move into position. Federal Army of the Cumberland (Thomas) begins to move east along the Western & Atlantic Railroad from Ringgold. Skirmishes east of Ringgold, near Tunnel Hill and Ringgold Gap; at Catoosa Springs, Red Clay, and Chickamauga Creek, Varnell's Station road (Prater's Mill), and Tunnel Hill
7	Army of the Tennessee (McPherson) moves south from Lee and Gordon's Mill along Taylor Ridge. Elements of the Army of the Cumberland attack Rebel skirmishers at Tunnel Hill and Varnell's Station. Skirmish at Nickajack Gap
8–11	General fighting along Rocky Face Ridge west of Dalton, specifically at Buzzard's Roost (Mill Creek) and Dug Gap
8–13	Demonstration against Resaca, with combat at Snake Creek Gap, Sugar Valley, and near Resaca
9	Army of the Tennessee moves towards the Western & Atlantic bridge near Resaca
	Army of the Ohio (Schofield) encounters Wheeler's Cavalry near Varnell
9–13	Demonstration against Dalton, with combat near Varnell's Station and Dalton
12	Johnston withdraws to Resaca
14–15	Battle of Resaca
15–18	Skirmishes in vicinity of Rome; engagement at Adairsville; action at Rome
18–19	Combat near Kingston and Cassville
20	Skirmish at Etowah River, near Cartersville
May 25 to June 5	Operations on the line of the Pumpkin Vine Creek, with combat at New Hope Church and Pickett's Mill
May 26 to June 1	Combat at Dallas
June 9–10	Skirmishes near Big Shanty and Stilesborough; at Calhoun
June 10 to July 3	Operations about Marietta, with combat at Pine Hill, Lost Mountain, Brush Mountain, Gilgal Church, Kennesaw Mountain, Kolb's Farm, Nickajack Creek, and other points
14	Lieutenant-General Leonidas Polk killed in action at Pine Mountain
24	Action at La Fayette

July 5–17	Operations on the line of the Chattahoochee River, with skirmishes at Howell's, Turner's, and Pace's Ferries, Isham's Ford, and other points
10–22	Rousseau's raid from Decatur, Alabama, to the West Point & Montgomery Railroad
18	General John Bell Hood supersedes General Joseph Eggleston Johnston in command of the Army of Tennessee
20	Battle of Peachtree Creek
21	Engagement at Bald (Leggett's) Hill
22	Battle of Atlanta. Major-General James B. McPherson killed in action
22–24	Garrard's raid to Covington
July 23 to August 25	Operations around Atlanta, including battle of Ezra Church (July 28), and Utoy Creek (August 6)
July 27–31	McCook's raid on the Atlanta & West Point and Macon & Western Railroads Garrard's raid to South River
July 27 to August 6	Stoneman's raid to Macon
August 10 to September 9	Wheeler's raid to North Georgia and East Tennessee
18–22	Kilpatrick's raid from Sandtown to Lovejoy's Station
August 26 to September 1	Operations at the Chattahoochee railroad bridge, and at Pace's and Turner's Ferries
August 29–31	Skirmishes near Red Oak and East Point; action at Flint River bridge; skirmish near Rough and Ready Station
August 31 to September 1	Battle of Jonesborough
September 2	Union occupation of Atlanta

OPPOSING PLANS

UNION PLANS

When Sherman met with his subordinate commanders in March 1864, to plan the upcoming campaign, he wrote that "General Johnston seemed to be acting purely on the defensive, so that we had time and leisure to take all our measures deliberately and fully." Johnston was obviously disinclined to come out of his reinforced position along Rocky Face Ridge to challenge a superior Union force. Sherman's detailed planning was aided by the fact that, in February, a sequence of events had occurred that provided Union forces an opportunity to reconnoiter Johnston's position.

On February 3, Sherman, then commanding the Army of the Tennessee at Vicksburg, marched 130 miles to Meridian, Mississippi, to tear up the railroad and destroy the Confederate arsenal there. Without Meridian's supply base and transportation system, it would be tremendously difficult for a Confederate force to mount an attack in the direction of the Mississippi River, thus freeing up additional Union manpower for the forthcoming campaigns.

Davis and Bragg directed Lieutenant-General Polk, commander of Confederate forces in Mississippi, to confront Sherman, with support from Lieutenant-General Hardee's Corps, currently in winter quarters at Dalton.

Sherman and his generals. Frank Blair was unavailable for the original photo, and had to be "added" by Mathew Brady, later. From left to right, Howard, Logan, Hazen, Sherman, Davis, Slocum, Mower, and Blair. (LOC)

Grant immediately saw an opportunity, and directed General Thomas and elements of the Army of Cumberland to advance south from Chattanooga, "to push the enemy as much as possible," hoping not only to test Johnston's defenses but also to force the Rebels to reconsider sending forces against Sherman. Between February 22 and 27, Thomas occupied Ringgold and Tunnel Hill, then assailed the Confederate fortifications at Mill Creek Gap, Dug Gap, and Crow Creek Valley. Polk, more

Snake Creek Gap. "Why these gaps were left unguarded, why a prompt effort was not made to hold Snake Creek Gap, I neither pretend to know nor venture to guess." Colonel W. C. P. Breckenridge, 9th Kentucky Cavalry. (Author's collection)

concerned that an attack on Mobile was imminent, turned back before reaching Meridian, and Hardee never departed Dalton. Thomas reported, "Inasmuch as it caused the recalling of re-enforcements sent to oppose General Sherman's expedition against Meridian, I concluded to withdraw my troops to the positions they had occupied previous to the reconnaissance."

Johnston refuted that Thomas's probing accomplished anything, but it did provide the Federal leadership with valuable intelligence. Sherman knew not only that a direct assault on Dalton was impractical, but also that there was a passage around Dalton via Snake Creek Gap, which led to Resaca, on the Western & Atlantic Railroad. With Resaca in Union hands, Johnston would be cut off from his line of communications to Atlanta and Richmond. He would thus have no choice but to fight or retreat.

Sherman planned accordingly. In a pattern he would follow, with a few notable exceptions, throughout the campaign, he would use the largest of his three armies, Thomas's Army of the Cumberland, to move against the center of Johnston's line on Rocky Face Ridge, hopefully holding the Rebels in place or forcing them to come out of their entrenchments, while his two smaller armies attacked the flanks. In particular, he would send McPherson's Army of the Tennessee south through Snake Creek Gap to seize the railroad at Resaca. Once Johnston's army was surrounded, and destroyed, the occupation of Atlanta would follow as a matter of course.

CONFEDERATE PLANS

Johnston was adamant that the best offense was a good defense. "I can see no other mode of taking the offensive here, than to beat the enemy when he advances, and then move forward." Davis and Bragg agreed with the strategy but argued that it should be Johnston maneuvering in an attempt to entice Sherman out of Chattanooga. "It is not deemed advisable to attempt the capture of the enemy's fortified positions by direct attack," wrote Bragg in March, "but to draw out, and then, if practicable, force him to battle in the open field." They proposed a link-up between Johnston and Longstreet, then in winter quarters in northeastern Tennessee, between Knoxville and Chattanooga. The capture of Nashville would be highly desirable, as would the necessity "of reclaiming the provision country of Tennessee and Kentucky."

Throughout the spring, while Johnston and Bragg debated courses of action, Johnston continued to express his concern about the discrepancy in manpower between his and Sherman's forces. Bragg stated that reinforcements were available and would be sent to him, "just as soon as you may be able to use them." Johnston wanted them immediately, but Bragg replied, "To throw them to the front now, would only impede the accumulation of supplies necessary for your march." Johnston persisted, expressing his doubts that Sherman would stand on the defensive. "We must have the *troops you name immediately.*" He concluded, "Give us *those troops*, and if we beat him, we follow, should he not advance, we will then be ready for the offensive."

Johnston prepared for the attack he knew was coming. "I supposed, from General Sherman's great superiority of numbers, that he intended to decide the contest by a battle as near his own and as far from our base as possible – that is to say, at Dalton." He wrote that the enemy, "even if beaten, had a safe refuge behind the fortified pass of Ringgold and in the

Federal camp at Chattanooga. Bragg's defeat at the battle of Chattanooga enabled Sherman to use it as the rallying point for his 100,000-man army, and the invasion of Georgia. (LOC)

fortress of Chattanooga. Our refuge in case of defeat was in Atlanta, 100 miles off, with three rivers intervening. Therefore, victory for us could not have been decisive, while defeat would have been utterly disastrous."

Johnston concentrated on fortifying his current position, while familiarizing himself with the area between Dalton and Atlanta. "My own operations, then and subsequently, we determined by the relative forces of the armies, and a higher estimate of the Northern soldiers than our Southern editors and politicians were accustomed to express, or even the Administration seemed to entertain." He believed in defense-in-depth. Each Confederate line was backed by an equally formidable one prepared in advance by his engineers. "So we held every position occupied until our communications were strongly threatened; then fell back only far enough to secure them. In the long run, he assured Richmond, he would "reduce the odds against us by partial engagements," prevent Sherman from sending reinforcements to Grant, and ultimately watch for opportunities to attack.

Fort Fisk. Johnston had six months to prepare, and used his time well. The steepness of the ascent to the heavily fortified positions wreaked havoc on the advancing Federal troops. (Author's collection)

OPPOSING COMMANDERS

UNION COMMANDERS

Major-General William Tecumseh Sherman. "You cannot qualify war in harsher terms than I will. War is cruelty, and you cannot refine it." Sherman to the Atlanta City Leaders, September 1864. (LOC)

Major-General William Tecumseh Sherman, known as "Cump" to his friends, finished sixth in a class of 43 at West Point in 1840. He saw action during the Second Seminole War; was stationed in Georgia, where he became familiar with the terrain that would have a bearing on his strategy during the campaign; and in 1859 became the first superintendent of what is, today, Louisiana State University. An ardent Unionist, he returned to the north in 1861, and led a regiment at Bull Run. Assigned to the Department of the Cumberland in Kentucky, he fell into a depression, questioning his leadership abilities, and had to take a leave of absence. He recovered enough to command a division under Grant in March 1862, and so distinguished himself at the battle of Shiloh in April 1862 that he was promoted to major-general. When Grant was reassigned in March 1864, Sherman inherited the command of the Western armies. "General Grant *is a great general*," he declared. "He stood by me when I was crazy, and I stood by him when he was drunk, and now, sir, we stand by each other always." After the war, he became Commanding General of the United States Army. At his funeral, General Joseph Johnston served as a pallbearer. When cautioned to put on his hat on account of the cold, Johnston replied, "If I were in his place, and he were standing in mine, he would not put on his hat." Johnston caught pneumonia and died one month later. Sherman was a pragmatist, conducting the Atlanta campaign with a firm consideration of his opponent's abilities, the battlefield terrain, his subordinates' capabilities, and a

commitment to avoiding unnecessary risk. "War is cruelty, and you cannot refine it."

Major-General George Henry Thomas, Sherman's roommate at West Point, was one of the few Southern-born officers to remain in the US Army at the outbreak of the war. Called variously "Old Tom," "Pap," and "Old Slow Trot," for his methodical ways, he was most affectionately known as "The Rock of Chickamauga," for his stubborn stand as the rest of the army abandoned the field during that battle in September 1863.

Major-General John McAllister Schofield was a graduate of the West Point class of 1853. Schofield led the smallest of Sherman's three armies, nominally a corps, and was considered to be "admirably qualified for the work before us." He served as Secretary of War under President Andrew Johnson, and received the Medal of Honor for his actions at the battle of Wilson's Creek in 1861.

Major-General James Birdseye McPherson was considered by both Grant and Sherman as the man most likely eventually to become commander of all Union armies. Sherman noted that he, "was universally liked, and had many noble qualities." His untimely death at the battle of Atlanta was deeply felt throughout the Union Army.

Major-General John McAllister Schofield. Once expelled from West Point, his dismissal was overturned on appeal. George Thomas was one of two officers to vote against the reinstatement. (LOC)

CONFEDERATE COMMANDERS

General Joseph Eggleston Johnston was the highest-ranking officer in the US Army to resign his commission at the outbreak of the Civil War. As such, he believed himself to be *the* senior officer in the Confederate Army in 1861, and was annoyed to find himself ranked fourth, behind Samuel Cooper, Albert Sidney Johnston, and Robert E. Lee. This began a war-long feud with Jefferson Davis, who declared that Johnston's commission as a brigadier-general in the US Army had been as a staff officer, and the others had been line officers. Johnston led the Department of Northern Virginia until he was wounded at the battle of Seven Pines, on May 31, 1862. He was famously succeeded by Robert E. Lee. Following his recovery, he was appointed commander of the Department of the West and was blamed by Davis for the surrender of Vicksburg, on July 4, 1863, by his subordinate, General John C. Pemberton. When General Braxton Bragg resigned his command of the Army of Tennessee after the battle of Chattanooga in November, Davis reluctantly appointed Johnston to the position. The Atlanta Campaign brought the feud between Johnston and Davis to a climax over Johnston's refusal to go on the offensive against Sherman's numerically superior forces, and he was replaced by John Bell Hood in July 1864. "We thought this was a struggle for independence," Mary Chestnut wrote in her diary. "Now it seems it is only a fight between Joe Johnston and Jeff Davis." Sherman valued Johnston as an

LEFT
General Joseph Eggleston Johnston. He considered himself the senior officer in the Confederate Army but was ranked fourth by Davis in a disagreement over line and staff officers. (LOC)

RIGHT
Lieutenant-General Leonidas Polk. Twice accused by Bragg of disobeying an order to attack (at Frankfort and Perryville, Kentucky), he was saved by his friendship with Davis. (LOC)

opponent, and commented that "the Confederate Government rendered us most valuable service," when Davis replaced him with Hood. After the war, Johnston's opinion of Davis, Hood, and others was clearly expressed in his *Narrative of Military Operations*.

Lieutenant-General John Bell Hood was widely renowned as a "fighter," and Sherman remarked that he was "bold even to rashness, and courageous in the extreme." Davis and Bragg believed that Hood's accession to command in Johnston's place would signal a positive change for the army. Hood could not be criticized for trying, and went on the attack three times in eight days, all unsuccessfully.

Lieutenant-General William Joseph Hardee, known as "Old Reliable," was the author of the 1855 manual, *Rifle and Light Infantry Tactics*, the standard textbook for Civil War officers on both sides. He was regarded as one of the finest corps commanders in the Army, and, when offered command of the Army of Tennessee in December 1863, before it was offered to Johnston, declined, believing his talents were better suited at corps level. When Hood succeeded Johnston, he believed that he should have again been considered for the post, and was highly critical of Hood's leadership.

Lieutenant-General Leonidas Polk, "The Bishop," was an Episcopal Bishop who was loved by his men, but was criticized most severely by Bragg for being sometimes slow to carry out orders. He saw no conflict between his religious and military duties, and, at the height of the campaign, baptized both Hood and Johnston. His death at Pine Mountain was considered second only to that of Stonewall Jackson's for its impact on Southern morale.

OPPOSING FORCES

UNION FORCES

At the outset of the campaign, Sherman reported his official strength to be 110,123 men. By September 1, it would stand at 81,758, but losses on the Confederate side ensured that he maintained a rough numerical superiority of no worse than 8:5 throughout the campaign. His primary disadvantage came from the fact that he was generally on the offensive in enemy territory and, the farther he advanced, the longer became his lines of supply and communication. This forced him to leave some level of manpower behind to ensure a continuous flow of materials to the front. The returns for April 10 show an aggregate of 180,000 soldiers present for duty on the muster rolls, reflecting the large number of troops required for garrison and supply-line duties.

Sherman's grand army consisted primarily of experienced soldiers who had been in the western theater for three years, but there was a major impediment to his ability to maintain such a veteran organization. Many of his regiments had organized in 1861 as three-year enlistees. To counteract the potential problem of large numbers of veterans leaving the army at the same time, the Federal government began offering 30-day furloughs to soldiers who re-enlisted for an additional three years. This incentive, and the paying of bounties to re-enlistees, helped maintain the level of experienced troops; however, many units were understrength until the furloughed soldiers returned.

Sherman's Army was well trained, well supplied, experienced, and accustomed to its foe after three years of brutal combat in the western theater. (LOC)

The largest of Sherman's organizations was the Army of the Cumberland, with three infantry and one cavalry corps. The unit was a veteran of the western campaigns, but, after its defeat at Chickamauga, fell out of favor with Grant, who replaced William Rosecrans with George Thomas prior to the battles around Chattanooga. Concerned about the unit's morale, he relegated it to the minor role of seizing the enemy's rifle pits at the

The battle of Missionary Ridge. Called "a soldier's battle," Union troops overran their objective, despite their commanders' attempts to stop them, and won a dramatic victory. (LOC)

"Sherman's neckties." Destruction of the railroad was a major pastime during the campaign. Piles of twisted iron became a symbol of attempts to prevent the tracks from being repaired. (LOC)

base of Missionary Ridge in order to pave the way for an advance by the Army of the Tennessee. In the heat of battle, four of the army's divisions overran the pits, stormed up the hill and routed the Confederate center. Major-General Gordon Granger, IV Corps commander, told Grant, "When those fellows get started all hell won't stop them."

One of Thomas's corps commanders was Major-General "Fighting Joe" Hooker, who had been sent west in the fall of 1863, with XI and XII Corps of the Army of the Potomac, to reinforce the Army of the Cumberland around Chattanooga. XI Corps had been on the ill-fated Union right flank at Chancellorsville and suffered the embarrassment of being overrun by Stonewall Jackson's flank attack on May 2, 1863. Two months later, the troops were again battered by Jubal Early's men on the first day at Gettysburg, but recovered to stop Early from taking East Cemetery Hill on July 2.

XII Corps had fared much better at Chancellorsville, retiring in good order from the Confederate attack, and at Gettysburg had participated in the desperate defense of Culp's Hill. Following their transfer west, they helped to open the "Cracker Line" that broke the siege of Chattanooga, and in November were commended for their victory at Lookout Mountain. In April, 1864, the two corps were combined and re-designated XX Corps of the Army of the Cumberland.

Sherman affectionately called the soldiers of his former command, the Army of the Tennessee, the "best men in America." Its three infantry corps had participated in virtually every major campaign in the western theater. Its most recent fighting had come during the Meridian Campaign, conducting what was later called a rehearsal for the March to the Sea. Sherman's troops destroyed over 100 miles of railroad, as well as numerous locomotives, railcars, bridges, and buildings. Sherman commented that the town itself, "with its depots, store-houses, arsenal, hospital, offices, hotels, and cantonments no longer exists."

In March, two divisions of XVI Corps and one from XVII Corps were detached, under the command of Brigadier-General A. J. Smith, to participate in Major-General Nathaniel Banks' Red River Campaign. The operation was the brainchild of Major-General Henry Halleck, the Union Army's Chief of Staff, in response to Lincoln's desire to see a Federal presence in Texas. Grant had planned to use Banks' Army of the Gulf against Mobile, Alabama, and he, along with Sherman and Banks, opposed the idea. Promised that Sherman's troops would be returned before the advance into Georgia, Grant reluctantly agreed. Banks led the expedition, which faltered almost from the start, and was soundly defeated at the battle of Sabine Crossroads on April 8, forcing his retreat. None of the three divisions participated directly in the Atlanta Campaign; however Smith led the two from XVI Corps to victory at the battle of Tupelo on July 15, protecting Sherman's supply lines in Mississippi. It was early June before XVII Corps, under the command of Major-General Frank Blair, joined Sherman.

The smallest of Sherman's commands was the Army of the Ohio, under Major-General John M. Schofield. It consisted of one corps, the XXIII, of three divisions, and a brigade of dismounted cavalry. Major-General George Stoneman was at Lexington, Kentucky collecting horses as the campaign began, but his cavalry division was added soon thereafter.

"The great question of the campaign was one of supplies," Sherman wrote. On April 6, he issued a general order limiting the use of the railroad to only those articles deemed essential to the army proper, forbidding any further use by civil traffic, and "requiring the commanders of posts within thirty miles of Nashville to haul out their own stores in wagons; requiring all troops destined for the front to march, and all beef-cattle to be driven on their own legs." When the citizenry of East Tennessee complained to Lincoln, the President asked Sherman if he could modify his order. Sherman responded that "a great campaign was impending, on which the fate of the nation hung," and Lincoln acquiesced.

Sherman's ultimate goal was a mobile, compact force, with limited "incumbrances [*sic*] and impedimenta." Officers would carry enough food and clothing for five days. Each regiment was limited to one wagon and one ambulance. The officers of each company were authorized one packhorse or mule. Division and brigade supply wagons were restricted to carrying food, ammunition, and clothing. Tents were forbidden, even for the officers, although Thomas insisted on his own, to which Sherman called his attention repeatedly to no effect. "I wanted to set the example," Sherman added, "and gradually to convert all parts of that army into a mobile machine, willing and able to start at a minute's notice, and to subsist on the scantiest food."

Thomas's camp at Ringgold. Despite Sherman's order that the army travel with a minimum of "impedimenta," Thomas "had a big wagon which could be converted into an office, and this we used to call 'Thomas's circus.'" (LOC)

CONFEDERATE FORCES

Johnston's army "at and near Dalton," on May 1, consisted of two infantry and one cavalry corps, totaling 43,887. Bragg had originally promised to send Longstreet's Corps of the Army of Northern Virginia, with its 16,000 men, and an additional 10,000 infantry under General P. G. T. Beauregard to Johnston, "as soon as you may be able to use them." Longstreet, wintering in northeast Tennessee after assisting Bragg at Chickamauga, was instead ordered to rejoin Lee in Virginia, and the force under Beauregard never materialized. Johnston did begin to receive elements of Lieutenant-General Leonidas Polk's Army of Mississippi, within days of the start of the campaign.

The Army of Tennessee was the largest Confederate field army in the western theater with a cadre of veteran soldiers commanded by some of the South's most experienced generals. The men were familiar with the Union soldiers they were about to face, having battled them at Stones River, Tullahoma, Chickamauga, and most recently, Chattanooga. They were heartened to be fighting under Johnston, having lost respect for Bragg, a feeling that permeated the organization.

The army's First Corps, under Lieutenant-General William J. Hardee, was more commonly referred to as "Hardee's Corps" in keeping with the Confederate tradition of designating units by the names of their commanders.

Lieutenant-General William Joseph Hardee resigned as commandant of cadets at West Point to join the Confederate Army. He wrote the tactics textbook used by commanders on both sides. (LOC)

It consisted of four divisions, supported by five battalions of artillery of mixed caliber and type.

The Second, or Hood's Corps, under Lieutenant-General John Bell Hood, consisted of three divisions, supported by four artillery battalions. At Chattanooga, the corps, then under Major-General John Breckenridge, had been in the center on Missionary Ridge when it was broken by Thomas's attack. Following reorganization, President Davis designated Hood as the new commander. Hood had fought at Gettysburg under Longstreet, where he was wounded, and at Chickamauga, where his division was instrumental in the rout of Rosecrans. He was wounded again, this time losing his right leg. Following his recovery, Hood set about restoring the unit's confidence as it prepared for the ensuing campaign.

Major-General Joseph Wheeler commanded Johnston's cavalry in four widely scattered divisions. His command would double in strength by June 10, as units were called in, or completed "recruiting horses." With the addition of Polk's army in May, Brigadier-General William H. Jackson's division joined the fight. Wheeler's command was highly experienced and fully capable of operating autonomously. In October 1863, the first "Wheeler's Raid" (the second would occur in August 1864) advanced into central Tennessee to destroy railroads and disrupt the Union supply lines. Following the Confederate Army's retreat from Chattanooga in November, Wheeler's divisions supported Major-General Patrick Cleburne's infantry at the battle of Ringgold Gap, effectively ending the Union Army's pursuit and enabling Bragg's army to stop near Dalton.

Polk's command consisted of three infantry divisions with supporting artillery, along with the previously mentioned cavalry under General Jackson, and was re-designated Polk's Corps of the Army of Tennessee after joining Johnston. Polk had been the commander at Meridian during Sherman's attack in February. As Sherman approached, Polk became convinced that the actual Federal target was Mobile, Alabama, and Meridian was only a feint. He pulled back before Sherman arrived, marching to Demopolis, Alabama, where he waited for an attack that never came.

In June, Johnston was reinforced by two brigades of infantry and one battalion of artillery from the Georgia Militia, totaling about 3,000 men. They were commanded by Major-General Gustavus W. Smith, who reported that, "although but poorly armed – very few having proper equipments, more than two-thirds without cartridge boxes – all performed well every service required." His one negative remark came from observing the men on the march; "men over fifty are not as a class fitted for military duty." Smith's more prominent claim to fame might have come from the fact that, as the senior officer on the field on May 31, 1862, he briefly took command of

Major-General Joseph Wheeler. The author of *Cavalry Tactics* conducted two significant raids into Tennessee, although the second, in August 1864, might have helped Sherman more than Hood. (LOC)

what would become the Army of Northern Virginia when then commander, General Johnston, was wounded at the battle of Seven Pines. Smith took ill, and was replaced the next day by Robert E. Lee.

Davis, Bragg, and Johnston reluctantly agreed that the men of the Army of Tennessee were in poor condition after the retreat from Chattanooga, although Davis and Bragg pressed for an early return to the offensive. Johnston was more pragmatic, referring to his new command as the "remnant of that which fought at Chickamauga and Missionary Ridge." Given five months to return the army to fighting condition, he concentrated on ensuring the basics of food, arms, and ammunition were in sufficient supply or adequately reachable. The army's primary shortages, which impacted Johnston's ability to take up the offensive, came from a need for artillery horses and field transportation. It was April before a representative of the Quartermaster's Department was sent to Dalton to supervise the acquisition of those resources. By the beginning of May, the horse problem had been solved, and the latter became unnecessary by the nature of the campaign.

ORDERS OF BATTLE

MILITARY DIVISION OF THE MISSISSIPPI MAJOR-GENERAL WILLIAM TECUMSEH SHERMAN

ARMY OF THE CUMBERLAND   **MAJ. GEN.**
GEORGE H. THOMAS

(61,651 Officers and Men, Infantry /2,551 Artillery/130 guns as of April 30)

IV CORPS   **MAJ. GEN. OLIVER O. HOWARD/MAJ.**
GEN. DAVID S. STANLEY

1st Division   **Maj. Gen. David S. Stanley/**
Brig. Gen. William Grose/Brig. Gen. Nathan Kimball

1st Brigade   Cruft/Kirby

21st Illinois/38th Illinois/31st Indiana/81st Indiana/1st Kentucky/2nd Kentucky/90th Ohio/101st Ohio/

2nd Brigade   Whitaker/Taylor

96th Illinois/115th Illinois/35th Indiana/84th Indiana/21st Kentucky/40th Ohio/51st Ohio/99th Ohio/

3rd Brigade   Grose

59th Illinois/75th Illinois/80th Illinois/84th Illinois/9th Indiana/30th Indiana/36th Indiana/77th Pennsylvania/

Artillery   Simonson (k)/McDowell (k)/Thomasson

5th Indiana Light/Battery B, Pennsylvania Light

2nd Division   **Brig. Gen. John Newton**

1st Brigade   F. Sherman/Kimball/Opdycke

36th Illinois/44th Illinois/73rd Illinois/74th Illinois/88th Illinois/28th Kentucky/2nd Missouri/15th Missouri/24th Wisconsin

2nd Brigade   Wagner/Blake

100th Illinois/40th Indiana/57th Indiana/26th Ohio/97th Ohio/

3rd Brigade   Harker (k)/Bradley

22nd Illinois/27th Illinois/42nd Illinois/51st Illinois/79th Illinois/3rd Kentucky/64th Ohio/65th Ohio/125th Ohio

Artillery   Aleshire/Goodspeed

Battery M, 1st Illinois Light/Battery A, 1st Ohio Light

3rd Division   **Brig. Gen. Thomas J. Wood**

1st Brigade   Willich (w)/Gibson

25th Illinois/35th Illinois/89th Illinois/32nd Indiana/8th Kansas/15th Ohio/49th Ohio/15th Wisconsin/

2nd Brigade   Hazen/Post

6th Indiana/5th Kentucky/6th Kentucky/23rd Kentucky/1st Ohio/6th Ohio/41st Ohio/93rd Ohio/124th Ohio

3rd Brigade   Beatty/Knefler

79th Indiana/86th Indiana/9th Kentucky/17th Kentucky/13th Ohio/19th Ohio/59th Ohio

Artillery   Bradley

Bridges' Illinois Light/6th Ohio Light

XIV CORPS   **MAJ. GEN. JOHN M. PALMER/BREVET**
MAJ. GEN. JEFFERSON C. DAVIS

1st Division Brig.   **Gen. Richard W. Johnson (w)/Brig. Gen.**
John H. King/Brig. Gen. William P. Carlin

1st Brigade   Carlin/A. McCook/Taylor

104th Illinois/42nd Indiana/88th Indiana/15th Kentucky/2nd Ohio/33rd Ohio/94th Ohio/10th Wisconsin/21st Wisconsin

2nd Brigade   King/Stoughton

11th Michigan/69th Ohio/15th US/16th US/18th US/19th US

3rd Brigade   Scribner/Moore

37th Indiana/38th Indiana/21st Ohio/74th Ohio/78th Pennsylvania/79th Pennsylvania/1st Wisconsin

Artillery   Drury

1st Illinois Light/Battery I, 1st Ohio

2nd Division   **Brig. Gen. Jefferson C. Davis/**
Brig. Gen. James D. Morgan

1st Brigade   Morgan/Lum

10th Illinois/16th Illinois/60th Illinois/10th Michigan/14th Michigan/17th New York

2nd Brigade   Mitchell

34th Illinois/78th Illinois/98th Ohio/108th Ohio/113th Ohio/121st Ohio

3rd Brigade   D. McCook (mw)/Harmon/Dilworth

85th Illinois/86th Illinois/110th Illinois/125th Illinois/22nd Indiana/52nd Ohio

Artillery   Barnett

2nd Illinois Light/5th Wisconsin Light

3rd Division   **Brig. Gen. Absalom Baird**

1st Brigade   Turchin/Walker

19th Illinois/24th Illinois/82nd Indiana/23rd Missouri/11th Ohio/17th Ohio/31st Ohio/89th Ohio/92nd Ohio

2nd Brigade   VanDerveer/Gleason

75th Indiana/87th Indiana/101st Indiana/2nd Minnesota/9th Ohio/35th Ohio/105th Ohio

3rd Brigade   Este

10th Indiana/74th Indiana/10th Kentucky/18th Kentucky/14th Ohio/38th Ohio

Artillery   Estep

7th Indiana Light/19th Indiana Light

XX CORPS   **MAJ. GEN. JOSEPH HOOKER/**
MAJ. GEN. HENRY W. SLOCUM

1st Division   **Brig. Gen. Alpheus S. Williams**

1st Brigade   Knipe

5th Connecticut/3rd Maryland/123rd New York/141st New York/46th Pennsylvania

2nd Brigade   Ruger

27th Indiana/2nd Massachusetts/13th New Jersey/107th New York/150th New York/3rd Wisconsin

3rd Brigade   Robinson

82nd Illinois/101st Illinois/45th New York/143rd New York/61st Ohio/82nd Ohio/31st Wisconsin

Artillery   Woodbury

Battery I, 1st New York Light/Battery M, 1st New York Light

2nd Division — Brig. Gen. John W. Geary

1st Brigade — Candy/Pardee
  5th Ohio/7th Ohio/29th Ohio/66th Ohio/28th Pennsylvania/147th Pennsylvania
2nd Brigade — Buschbeck/Lockman
  33rd New Jersey/119th New York/134th New York/154th New York/27th Pennsylvania/73rd Pennsylvania/109th Pennsylvania
3rd Brigade — Ireland (w)/Cobham
  60th New York/78th New York/102nd New York/137th New York/149th New York/11th Pennsylvania/29th Pennsylvania
  Artillery Wheeler (k)/Aleshire
  13th New York Light/Battery E, Pennsylvania Light

3rd Division — Maj. Gen. Daniel Butterfield/ Brig. Gen. William T. Ward

1st Brigade — Ward
  102nd Illinois/105th Illinois/129th Illinois/70th Indiana/79th Ohio
  2nd Brigade Coburn
  20th Connecticut/33rd Indiana/85th Indiana/19th Michigan/22nd Wisconsin
3rd Brigade — J. Wood
  20th Connecticut/33rd Massachusetts/136th New York/55th Ohio/73rd Ohio/26th Wisconsin
Artillery — Gary
  Battery I, 1st Michigan Light/Battery C, 1st Ohio Light

CAVALRY CORPS — BRIG. GEN. WASHINGTON ELLIOTT

(8,826)

1st Division — Brig. Gen. Edward M. McCook

1st Brigade — Dorr
  8th Iowa/4th Kentucky/2nd Michigan/1st Tennessee/1st Wisconsin
2nd Brigade — LaGrange/Stewart/Lamson
  2nd Indiana/4th Indiana
3rd Brigade — Watkins
  4th Kentucky/6th Kentucky
  Artillery Rippetoe/Beck
  18th Indiana Horse Artillery

2nd Division — Brig. Gen. Kenner Garrard

1st Brigade — Minty
  4th Michigan/7th Pennsylvania/4th US
2nd Brigade — Long
  1st Ohio/3rd Ohio/4th Ohio
3rd Brigade — Wilder
  98th Illinois/123rd Illinois/17th Indiana/72nd Indiana
Artillery
  Chicago Board of Trade Artillery

3rd Division — Brig. Gen. Judson Kilpatrick/Col. Eli Murray

1st Brigade — Klein
  3rd Indiana/5th Iowa
2nd Brigade — Smith
  8th Indiana/2nd Kentucky/10th Ohio
3rd Brigade — Murray/Adkins
  92nd Illinois/3rd Kentucky/5th Kentucky
Artillery
  10th Wisconsin

ARMY OF THE TENNESSEE — MAJ. GEN. JAMES B. MCPHERSON (K)/ MAJ. GEN. OLIVER O. HOWARD

(22,308 Infantry/1,394 Artillery/96 guns (excludes XVII Corps))

XV CORPS — MAJ. GEN. JOHN A. LOGAN

1st Division — Brig. Gen. Peter J. Osterhaus/Brig. Gen. Charles A. Woods

1st Brigade — C. Woods/M. Smith
  26th Iowa/30th Iowa/27th Missouri/76th Ohio
2nd Brigade — Williamson
  4th Iowa/9th Iowa/25th Iowa/31st Iowa
3rd Brigade — Wangelin
  3rd Missouri/12th Missouri/17th Missouri/29th Missouri/31st Missouri//32nd Missouri
Artillery — Landgraeber
  Battery F, 2nd Missouri Light/4th Ohio Light

2nd Division — Brig. Gen. Morgan L. Smith/ Brig. Gen. G William B. Hazen

1st Brigade — G. Smith/T. Jones
  55th Illinois/111th Illinois/116th Illinois/127th Illinois/6th Missouri/8th Missouri/57th Ohio
2nd Brigade — Lightburn/W. Jones
  83rd Indiana/30th Ohio/37th Ohio/47th Ohio/53rd Ohio/54th Ohio
Artillery — DeGress
  Batteries A, B, & H, 1st Illinois Light

3rd Division — Brig. Gen. John E. Smith

1st Brigade — Alexander
  63rd Illinois/48th Indiana/59th Indiana/4th Minnesota/18th Wisconsin
2nd Brigade — Raum
  13th Illinois/56th Illinois/17th Iowa/10th Missouri/24th Missouri/80th Ohio
3rd Brigade — Matthies/Dean/Banbury
  93rd Illinois/5th Iowa/10th Iowa/26th Missouri
Artillery — Dillon
  6th & 12th Batteries Wisconsin Light

4th Division — Brig. Gen. William Harrow

1st Brigade — R. Williams/Oliver
  26th Illinois/90th Illinois/12th Indiana/100th Indiana
2nd Brigade — Brig. Gen. Charles C. Walcutt
  40th Illinois/103rd Illinois/97th Indiana/6th Iowa/46th Ohio
3rd Brigade — Oliver
  48th Illinois/99th Indiana/15th Michigan/53rd Ohio/70th Ohio
Artillery — Griffiths/Burton
  Battery F, 1st Illinois Light/1st Battery, Iowa Light

XVI CORPS — MAJ. GEN. GRENVILLE M. DODGE (W)/ BRIG. GEN. THOMAS E. G. RANSOM

2nd Division — Brig. Gen. Thomas W. Sweeny/Brig. Gen. John M. Corse

1st Brigade — Rice
  52nd Illinois/66th Indiana/2nd Iowa/7th Iowa
2nd Brigade — Burke (mw)/Adams/Mersy
  9th Illinois Mounted Infantry/12th Illinois/66th Illinois (Western Sharpshooters)/81st Ohio

3rd Brigade   Bane/VanDerveer/Cummings/Rowet
7th Illinois/50th Illinois/57th Illinois/39th Iowa
Artillery   Welker
Battery B, 1st Michigan Light/Battery H, 1st Missouri Light/
Battery I, 1st Missouri Light

4th Division   **Brig. Gen. James C. Veatch/**
Brig. Gen. John W. Fuller
1st Brigade   Fuller/McDowell
64th Illinois/8th Missouri/27th Ohio/39th Ohio
2nd Brigade   Sprague
35th New Jersey/43rd Ohio/63rd Ohio/25th Wisconsin
3rd Brigade   Howe/Grower/Tillson
10th Illinois/25th Indiana/17th New York/32nd Wisconsin
Artillery   Burrows/Robinson
Battery C, 1st Michigan Light/14th Ohio Light/Battery F, 2nd US

XVII CORPS   MAJ. GEN. FRANCIS P. BLAIR, JR.

(8,767 Infantry/921 Artillery as of May 31)

3rd Division   **Brig. Gen. Mortimer D. Leggett/**
Brig. Gen. Charles R. Woods
1st Brigade   Force (w)/Bryant
20th Illinois/30th Illinois/31st Illinois/45th Illinois/16th Wisconsin
2nd Brigade   Scott/Wiles
20th Ohio/32nd Ohio/68th Ohio/78th Ohio
3rd Brigade   Malloy
17th Wisconsin/Worden's Battalion
Artillery   W. Williams
Battery D, 1st Illinois Light/Battery H, 1st Michigan Light/
3rd Ohio Light

4th Division   **Brig. Gen. Walter Q. Gresham (w)/**
Brig. Gen. Giles A. Smith
1st Brigade   Sanderson/Potts
32nd Illinois/23rd Indiana/53rd Indiana/3rd Iowa/12th Wisconsin
2nd Brigade   Rogers/Pugh/Logan
14th Illinois/15th Illinois/41st Illinois/53rd Illinois
3rd Brigade   Hall/Belknap
11th Iowa/13th Iowa/15th Iowa/16th Iowa
Artillery   Spear/Clayton
Battery F, 2nd Illinois Light/Battery C, 1st Missouri Light/1st
Minnesota/10th Ohio Light/15th Ohio Light

ARMY OF THE OHIO   MAJ. GEN. JOHN M. SCHOFIELD

(9,262 Infantry/592 Artillery/2,951 Cavalry/28 guns)

XXIII CORPS   MAJ. GEN. JOHN M. SCHOFIELD

1st Division   **Brig. Gen. Alvin P. Hovey**
1st Brigade   Barter
120th Indiana/124th Indiana/128th Indiana
2nd Brigade   McQuiston/Swaine
123rd Indiana/129th Indiana/130th Indiana/99th Ohio
Artillery
23rd Indiana Light/24th Indiana Light
2nd Division   **Brig. Gen. Henry M. Judah/**
Brig. Gen. Milo S. Hascall
1st Brigade   McLean/Cooper
80th Indiana/91st Indiana/13th Kentucky/25th Michigan/3rd
Tennessee/6th Tennessee
2nd Brigade   Hascall/Bond/Hobson
107th Illinois/80th Indiana/23rd Michigan/45th Ohio/111th
Ohio/118th Ohio
3rd Brigade   Strickland
14th Kentucky/20th Kentucky/27th Kentucky/50th Ohio
Artillery   Shields
22nd Indiana Light/Battery F, 1st Michigan Light/19th Ohio Light
3rd Division   **Brig. Gen. Jacob D. Cox**
1st Brigade   Reilly
112th Illinois/16th Kentucky/100th Ohio/104th Ohio/8th Tennessee
2nd Brigade   Manson (w)/Casement/Cameron
65th Illinois/63rd Indiana/65th Indiana/24th Kentucky/103rd
Ohio/5th Tennessee
3rd Brigade McLean/Byrd/Stiles
11th Kentucky/12th Kentucky/1st Tennessee/5th Tennessee
Dismounted Cavalry Crittenden
16th Illinois/12th Kentucky
Artillery   Wells
15th Indiana Light/Battery D, 1st Ohio Light
Cavalry Division   **Maj. Gen. George Stoneman**
1st Brigade   I. Garrard
9th Michigan/7th Ohio
2nd Brigade   Biddle/Butler
16th Illinois/5th Indiana/6th Indiana/12th Kentucky
3rd Brigade   Capron
14th Illinois/8th Michigan/McLaughlin's Ohio Squadron
Independent Brigade   Holeman/Adams
1st Kentucky/11th Kentucky
Artillery   Hardy/Allen
24th Indiana

ARMY OF TENNESSEE GEN. JOSEPH EGGLESTON JOHNSTON/GEN. JOHN BELL HOOD (43,887/120 GUNS)

HARDEE'S CORPS   LT. GEN. WILLIAM J. HARDEE

Cheatham's Division   **Maj. Gen. Benjamin F. Cheatham/**
Brig. Gen. George E. Maney/
Brig. Gen. John C. Carter

Maney's Brigade   Porter
4th Confederate/1st & 27th Tennessee/6th & 9th Tennessee/41st
Tennessee/50th Tennessee/24th Tennessee Battalion

Strahl's Brigade — Strahl

    4th & 5th Tennessee/19th Tennessee/24th Tennessee/31st Tennessee/33rd Tennessee

Wright's Brigade — Carter

    8th Tennessee/16th Tennessee/28th Tennessee/38th Tennessee/51st & 52nd Tennessee

Vaughn's Brigade — Vaughn/Magevney

    11th Tennessee/12th & 47th Tennessee/13th & 154th Tennessee/29th Tennessee

Cleburne's Division — Maj. Gen. Patrick R. Cleburne

Polk's Brigade — Lucius Polk

    1st and 15th Arkansas/2nd Tennessee/35th & 48th Tennessee/5th Confederate

Govan's Brigade — Govan

    2nd & 24th Arkansas/5th & 13th Arkansas/6th & 7th Arkansas/8th & 19th Arkansas/3rd Confederate

Lowrey's Brigade — Lowrey

    16th Alabama/33rd Alabama/45th Alabama/32nd Mississippi/45th Mississippi

Granbury's Brigade — Granbury

    6th Texas & 15th Texas Cavalry (dismounted)/7th Texas/10th Texas/17th & 18th Texas Cavalry (dismounted)/ 24th & 25th Texas Cavalry (dismounted)

Bate's Division — Maj. Gen. G. William B. Bate

Smith's/Tyler's Brigade — Smith

    37th Georgia/4th Georgia Battalion Sharpshooters/10th Tennessee/15th & 37th Tennessee/20th Tennessee/ 30th Tennessee

Lewis' Brigade — Lewis

    2nd Kentucky/4th Kentucky/5th Kentucky/6th Kentucky/9th Kentucky

Finley's Florida Brigade — Finley

    1st Florida Cavalry (dismounted) & 3rd Florida/1st & 4th Florida/6th Florida/7th Florida

Jackson's Brigade — Jackson

    1st Georgia Battalion Sharpshooters/25th Georgia/29th Georgia/30th Georgia/66th Georgia

Walker's Division — Maj. Gen. William H. T. Walker*

Mercer's Brigade — Mercer

    1st Georgia/54th Georgia/57th Georgia/63rd Georgia

Gist's Georgia Brigade — Gist

    8th Georgia Battalion/46th Georgia/16th South Carolina/24th South Carolina

Jackson's Brigade — Jackson

    47th Georgia/65th Georgia/5th Mississippi/8th Mississippi/2nd Georgia Battalion Sharpshooters/1st Confederate

Stevens' Georgia Brigade — Stevens

    1st Georgia Battalion Sharpshooters/25th Georgia/29th Georgia/30th Georgia/66th Georgia/26th Georgia Battalion

* Walker's division broken up Jul 24. Brigades assigned to other divisions of this corps

HOOD'S/LEE'S CORPS — LT. GEN. JOHN BELL HOOD/ MAJ. GEN. BENJAMIN F. CHEATHAM/ LT. GEN. STEPHEN D. LEE

Hindman's/Anderson's Division — Maj. Gen. Thomas C. Hindman (w)/Maj. Gen. Patton Anderson

Deas' Alabama Brigade — Deas/Coltart

    19th Alabama/22nd Alabama/25th Alabama/39th Alabama/50th Alabama/17th Alabama Battalion Sharpshooters

Manigault's Brigade — Manigault

    24th Alabama/28th Alabama/34th Alabama/10th South Carolina/19th South Carolina

Wathall's/Brantly's Mississippi Brigade — Walthall/Benton

    24th & 27th Mississippi/29th & 30th Mississippi/34th Mississippi

Tucker's/Sharp's Mississippi Brigade — Tucker/Sharp

    7th Mississippi/9th Mississippi/10th Mississippi/41st Mississippi/44th Mississippi/9th Mississippi Battalion Sharpshooters

Stevenson's Division — Maj. Gen. Carter L. Stevenson

Brown's Brigade — Brown

    3rd Tennessee/18th Tennessee/26th Tennessee/32nd Tennessee/45th & 23rd Tennessee

Cumming's Georgia Brigade — Cumming

    34th Georgia/36th Georgia/39th Georgia/56th Georgia/2nd Georgia State Line

Reynolds' Brigade — Reynolds

    58th North Carolina/60th North Carolina/54th Virginia/63rd Virginia

Pettus' Alabama Brigade — Pettus

    20th Alabama/23rd Alabama/30th Alabama/31st Alabama/46th Alabama

Stewart's/Clayton's Division — Maj. Gen. Alexander P. Stewart/ Maj. Gen. Henry D. Clayton

Stovall's Georgia Brigade — Stovall/Johnson

    40th Georgia/41st Georgia/42nd Georgia/43rd Georgia/52nd Georgia/1st Georgia State Line

Clayton's Brigade — Clayton/Holtzclaw

    18th Alabama/32nd & 58th Alabama/36th Alabama/38th Alabama

Gibson's/Holtzclaw's Brigade — Gibson

    1st Louisiana/13th Louisiana/16th & 25th Louisiana/19th Louisiana/20th Louisiana/4th Louisiana Battalion Sharpshooters/14th (Austin's) Louisiana Battalion Sharpshooters

Baker's Alabama Brigade — Baker

    37th Alabama/40th Alabama/42nd Alabama/54th Alabama

POLK'S/STEWART'S CORPS (ARMY OF MISSISSIPPI) LT. GEN. LEONIDAS POLK (K)/LT. GEN. ALEXANDER P. STEWART (14,450/50 GUNS)

Loring's Division — Maj. Gen. William W. Loring/ Brig. Gen. Winfield S. Featherston

1st Brigade — Featherston/Lowry

    3rd Mississippi/22nd Mississippi/31st Mississippi/33rd Mississippi/40th Mississippi/1st Mississippi Sharpshooters

2nd Brigade — Adams

    6th Mississippi/14th Mississippi/15th Mississippi/20th Mississippi/23rd Mississippi/43rd Mississippi

3rd Brigade — Scott

    27th Alabama/35th Alabama/49th Alabama/55th Alabama/57th Alabama/12th Louisiana

French's Division — Maj. Gen. Samuel G. French

1st Brigade — Ector/Young

    29th North Carolina/39th North Carolina/9th Texas/10th Texas Cavalry (dismounted)/14th Texas Cavalry (dismounted)/32nd Texas Cavalry (dismounted)

2nd Brigade   Cockrell/Gates
    1st & 4th Missouri/2nd & 6th Missouri/3rd & 5th Missouri/1st &
    3rd Missouri Cavalry (dismounted)
3rd Brigade   Sears/Barry
    4th Mississippi/35th Mississippi/36th Mississippi/39th
    Mississippi/46th Mississippi/7th Mississippi Battalion

Walthall's Division   **Maj. Gen. Edward C. Walthall**
1st Brigade   Reynolds
    1st Arkansas Mounted Rifles (dismounted)/2nd Arkansas
    Mounted Rifles (dismounted)/4th Arkansas/9th Arkansas/25th
    Arkansas
2nd Brigade   Cantey/O'Neal
    17th Alabama/26th Alabama/29th Alabama/37th Mississippi
3rd Brigade   Quarles
    1st Alabama/4th Louisiana/30th Louisiana/42nd
    Tennessee/46th & 55th Tennessee/48th Tennessee/49th
    Tennessee/53rd Tennessee

ARTILLERY   **BRIG. GEN. FRANCIS A. SHOUP**
Hardee's Corps Artillery   **Col. Melanchthon Smith**
Hoxton's Battalion   Hoxton
    Phelan's Alabama/Perry's Florida/Turner's Mississippi Batteries
Hotchkiss' Battalion   Hotchkiss
    Semple's (Goldwaite's) Alabama/Key's Arkansas/Warren's Light
    (Shannon's Mississippi) Batteries
Martin's Battalion   Martin
    Howell's Georgia/Bledsoe's Missouri/Ferguson's (Beauregard's)
    South Carolina Batteries
Cobb's Battalion   Cobb
    Gracey's (Cobb's) Kentucky/Slocomb's Washington Louisiana
    Light/Mebane's (Johnston's) Tennessee Batteries
Palmer's Battalion   Palmer
    Lumsden's Alabama/Anderson's Georgia/Havis' Georgia
    Batteries
Hood's/Lee's Corps Artillery   **Col. Robert F. Beckham**
Courtney's Battalion   Courtney
    Dent's Alabama/Garrity's Alabama/Douglas' Texas Batteries
Eldridge's Battalion   Eldridge
    Oliver's Eufaula Alabama/Fenner's Louisiana/Stanford's
    Mississippi Batteries
Johnston's Battalion   Johnston
    Corput's Cherokee Georgia/Rowan's (Stephen's) Georgia Light/
    Marshall's Tennessee Batteries
Williams' Battalion   Williams
    Kolb's Barbour Alabama/Darden's Jefferson Mississippi/Jefress'
    Virginia Batteries
Polk's/Stewart's Corps Artillery   **Lt. Col. Samuel C. Williams**
Myrick's Battalion   Myrick
    Bouanchaud's Louisiana/Cowan's Mississippi/Barry's Lookout
    Tennessee Batteries

Storrs' Battalion   Storrs
    Ward's Alabama/Hoskins' Mississippi/Guibor's Missouri Batteries
Preston's Battalion   Preston
    Tarrant's Alabama/Lovelace's/Gid Nelson's Selma Alabama/Yates'
    Mississippi Batteries
Waddell's Battalion   Waddell
    Bellamy's Alabama/Emery's Alabama/Barrett's Missouri Batteries

CAVALRY CORPS   **MAJ. GEN. JOSEPH WHEELER**
(8,656)
Martin's Division   **Maj. Gen. William T. Martin**
Morgan's/Allen's Brigade   Morgan/Allen
    1st Alabama/3rd Alabama/4th Alabama/5th Alabama/51st
    Alabama
Iverson's Brigade   Iverson
    1st Georgia/2nd Georgia/3rd Georgia/4th Georgia/6th Georgia
Kelly's Division   **Brig. Gen. John H. Kelly**
Allen's/Anderson's Brigade   Allen/Anderson
    3rd Confederate/8th Confederate/10th Confederate/12th
    Confederate/5th Georgia
Dibrell's Brigade   Dibrell
    4th Tennessee/8th Tennessee/9th Tennessee/10th
    Tennessee/11th Tennessee
Hannon's Brigade   Hannon
    24th Alabama Battalion/53rd Alabama
Humes' Division   **Brig. Gen. William Y. C. Humes**
Hume's/Ashby's Brigade   Wheeler/Ashby
    1st Tennessee/2nd Tennessee/5th Tennessee/9th Tennessee
Harrison's Brigade   Harrison
    3rd Arkansas/4th Tennessee/8th Texas/11th Texas
Grigsby's/Williams' Brigade   Grigsby/Williams
    1st Kentucky/2nd Kentucky/9th Kentucky/Allison's Tennessee
    Squadron
Jackson's Division   **Brig. Gen. William Hicks Jackson**
Armstrong's Brigade   Armstrong
    1st Mississippi/2nd Mississippi/28th Mississippi/Ballentine's
    Mississippi Regiment
Ross' Texas Brigade   Ross
    1st Texas Legion/3rd Texas/6th Texas/9th Texas
Ferguson's Brigade   Brig. Gen. Samuel W. Ferguson
    2nd Alabama/56th Alabama/9th Mississippi/11th
    Mississippi/12th Mississippi Battalion
Jackson's Division Artillery   Waites
    Croft's Columbus Georgia/King's Missouri/Waddell's South
    Carolina Batteries
Wheeler's Horse Artillery   Robertson
    Callaway's Arkansas/Huggin's Tennessee/White's Tennessee
    Battery/Davis' Georgia/Huwald's Tennessee Batteries

THE CAMPAIGN

OPENING MOVES, APRIL 25 TO MAY 6, 1864

On April 25, 1864, Major-General William Tecumseh Sherman issued Special Order No. 35, to "the armies on the line of the Tennessee for the purpose of war." He designated Major-General George H. Thomas's Army of the Cumberland as the center of the advance, with Major-General John M. Schofield's Army of the Ohio on the left wing, and Major-General James B. McPherson and the Army of the Tennessee on the right. Sherman's challenge was to dislodge General Joseph Eggleston Johnston and the Confederate Army of Tennessee from Rocky Face Ridge in northwest Georgia, defeat them on ground of his own choosing, and destroy the Rebel supply center at Atlanta.

"In the morning of the 2d May," Johnston wrote, "a close reconnaissance of our outpost at Tunnel Hill was made under the protection of a strong body of infantry, cavalry, and artillery." Johnston telegraphed General Braxton Bragg, President Jefferson Davis's military adviser that, "the beginning of an active campaign was imminent." Bragg replied that Johnston was probably "deceived."

If Johnston was to be deceived about anything, Sherman hoped that it was about the design of the Federal approach. Sherman had no illusions about the strength of the Rebel line. "The position was very strong, and I knew that such a general as my antagonist (Jos. Johnston), who had been there six months, had fortified it to the maximum."

RIGHT
Mill Creek Gap. Both commanders were fully aware of the strategic value of the most direct route to Dalton, Johnston's headquarters, and hub for the Western & Atlantic Railroad. (Author's collection)

LEFT
Sherman moves south. In a telegram to Grant, Sherman stated "I can make this march, and I will make Georgia howl." (LOC)

Johnston believed that Sherman had no choice but to go over or through Rocky Face Ridge. If his task was to advance on Atlanta, Sherman needed the rail line, which crossed the ridge at Mill Creek Gap, to supply his army; and if his objective was Johnston's army, there it sat, well entrenched along the steep face of the escarpment. Sherman would have to follow the line of the Western & Atlantic Railroad from Chattanooga through Tunnel Hill to Dalton.

With respect to the ridge itself, there were three routes that provided Sherman direct access to Dalton. Lieutenant-General John Bell Hood's corps held Johnston's right flank, covering the rail line from Cleveland, Tennessee. From there, the Confederate front stretched across the northern end of the ridge, before arcing south along its western crest to Mill Creek Gap. Lieutenant-General William J. Hardee's corps held the left flank west of Dalton extending from Mill Creek Gap towards Dug Gap, which was 4 miles to the south, and initially unguarded.

Sherman "had no intention to attack the position seriously in front." He directed Thomas and Schofield, "merely to press strongly at all points," while McPherson made a wide flanking maneuver to the south. Eight miles southwest of Dalton, McPherson would pass through Snake Creek Gap, a narrow defile that would place him 5 miles west of the railroad at Resaca, the Confederate lifeline to Atlanta. With that line in Federal control, Johnston would be forced "to evacuate his position at Dalton altogether." The plan was a good one, but, like any military operation, depended on the commander on the ground to carry it out.

On April 28, Sherman moved his headquarters from Nashville to Chattanooga, and prepared to take the field in person. Thomas began the advance on May 2, with Tunnel Hill as his first objective. Major-General John Palmer led XIV Corps to Ringgold, 6 miles northwest of the tunnel, with Major-General Oliver O. Howard and IV Corps moving from Cleveland, Tennessee to Catoosa Springs, 3 miles to the east. Major-General "Fighting Joe" Hooker led XX Corps on the right flank, through Nickajack Gap, 5 miles southwest of Tunnel Hill. His movement served to screen McPherson's army to his right. All three corps were in position by the 5th.

Johnston ordered his cavalry, under Major-General Joseph Wheeler, to Tunnel Hill, while notifying Richmond that "the concurring reports of every scout" indicate that the enemy "will immediately attack with his united forces." Reluctantly, President Davis directed Lieutenant-General Leonidas Polk to move his Army of Mississippi the 200 miles from Demopolis, Alabama to Rome, Georgia, placing them within supporting distance of Johnston, 45 miles from Dalton

ROCKY FACE RIDGE, MAY 7–13, 1864

The offensive started better than Sherman had anticipated. The topography of northwest Georgia, a series of steep ridges and deep valleys, favored the defensive. Rocky Face Ridge was a formidable position, with Tunnel Hill, 3 miles to the north-northwest, the most direct route to it. There, the Western & Atlantic Railroad tunnel, which gave the hill and the nearby town its name, cut a 1,477-foot hole through the Chetoogeta Mountain. Sherman was "agreeably surprised" to find Tunnel Hill not only lightly guarded, but undamaged.

At daylight on May 7, Brigadier-General Jefferson C. Davis (no relation to the Confederate President), 2nd Division, XIV Corps, marched from Ringgold. Major James T. Holmes, of the 52nd Ohio Infantry, reported that "the skirmishers struck the enemy's vedettes at a distance of two miles from Ringgold and a desultory firing was kept up until within a mile of Tunnel Hill, when a brisk skirmish took place, the enemy's force consisting of 50 to 100 cavalry or mounted infantry." The defenders were Wheeler's men, who were driven back in the face of overwhelming force.

To the southwest, the Army of the Tennessee was reaching its first objective. McPherson led two of his three corps, XV and XVI (XVII would arrive in June), south from Chattanooga on the 5th. Passing through Gordon's Mill, they were on the far side of Taylor's Ridge, 10 miles west of Dalton, on the 7th. It would take another two days to reach Snake Creek Gap. Not only was the pass screened from Johnston's forces, but, during Thomas's reconnaissance-in-force in February, had been unguarded. McPherson would emerge on Johnston's left flank, which, at the moment, was focused on Thomas's troops emerging from Tunnel Hill.

Johnston was not impressed with the Federal attack. "Its progress was so slow, that the Confederates were not driven from Tunnel Hill until eleven o'clock A.M.," he wrote, "or to Mill-Creek Gap until three P.M." Slow or not, by late afternoon, three Federal corps, XXIII, IV, and XIV, were aligned in front of the ridge.

For the next several days, Thomas and Schofield pushed at the Confederate line, looking for weaknesses. They did not find many, and the Union troops quickly learned how tough an assault on the fortified Confederate position would be. Harker's brigade of Newton's 2nd Division, IV Corps, climbed the northern extremity of Rocky Face Ridge just after daylight on the 8th. Colonel Emerson Opdycke's 125th Ohio Infantry was ordered to "effect a lodgment" on the summit. "The ridge is 500 or 600 feet high, and the crest so narrow as to render it impossible for more than four men to march abreast upon it," Opdycke noted. With great effort, they drove the rebel skirmishers back far enough to establish a signal station and open communications with Tunnel Hill. "We had a plain view of the enemy's works and batteries, and could see Dalton," Opdycke concluded, "the importance of it as a point of observation was apparent.

By nightfall, the brigade had covered a distance of barely three-quarters of a mile. Overnight, one artillery piece was brought up, and, in the morning, the attack continued. "The

Tunnel Hill. The tunnel, completed in 1850, is 1,477 feet long. Had the Rebels destroyed it, Sherman's supply line, and the campaign itself, could have been seriously disrupted. (Author's collection)

The attack on Rocky Face Ridge. General Newton, whose division was tasked with taking the ridge, reported, "This day's operations demonstrated the enemy's position on the slope and crest to be impregnable." (LOC)

The Fight at Dug Gap. One member of the 29th Ohio noted that "the slanted ground was covered with a layer of flat, loose rock, making upward motion not unlike scaling the sides of a church steeple on which the shingles had not been nailed down." (LOC)

whole extent of the ridge occupied by us amounted to about a mile and three quarters," Newton wrote. "As each enemy position was crossed, the Confederate troops fell back to another, more secure line."

At Mill Creek Gap, three Federal divisions hit the center of Hardee's line, reaching the mouth of the gap, but advancing no farther. The approach was covered by artillery, and the Rebels had dammed Mill Creek, flooding the road. Detachments of the 34th Illinois made three increasingly aggressive, but futile, attempts to un-dam the creek. The flooded gap, along with the surrounding fortifications, completely stymied the Federal attack.

Farther south, at Dug Gap, the result was much the same. Colonel W. C. P. Breckenridge and the 9th Kentucky Cavalry, part of the force that had been driven from Tunnel Hill on the 7th, rode to Babb's Settlement, "to ascertain the movements of the enemy. Large bodies of troops were discovered on all roads leading south. Elements of Hooker's Corps were marching east toward Dug Gap." They also noted columns of McPherson's troops, but reported that "until McPherson reached Villanow it was only conjecture as to his course." The more immediate concern was defending Dug Gap against "forces too large to be either resisted or developed by the 9th Kentucky."

At 3.00pm on the 8th, Geary's 2nd Division of Hooker's Corps was ordered to "make a strong demonstration and, if possible, carry the rebel positions." Six regiments of Adolphus Buschbeck's 2nd Brigade, followed by two regiments of Charles Candy's 1st Brigade, roughly 3,000 men, "determined to carry the heights, and so far succeeded that the greater part of the advance gained the crest," but their hold on it was temporary.

By then, the remainder of Colonel Warren Grigsby's cavalry brigade had joined the 9th Kentucky. Grigsby's 800 cavalrymen were reinforced by a mere 250 from the 1st and 2nd Arkansas regiments of Williamson's brigade who had been rushed to the gap, and together, they pushed back the initial attack, and four subsequent attempts. In addition to their musket fire, the Rebels rolled large boulders down the steep hill. By nightfall, Granbury's Brigade of Cleburne's Division had joined them, but "the assault was over." According to Breckenridge, "Hooker had failed in his part of the mission." The Union troops were more than certain that Geary had achieved his objective of a "demonstration," albeit at a cost of one in three officers and men. Geary deemed any further loss of life unnecessary and "retired my command slowly and in good order." Casualties on the Confederate side, according to Breckenridge, were "in killed and wounded not a score."

Grigsby's cavalry had no sooner retired from the Dug Gap line when the order came to ride to Snake Creek Gap. They were told to look for a company of Georgia troops on picket duty at or near its eastern outlet. "The night was dark, the road rough and unfamiliar, and it was difficult to find guides," Colonel Breckenridge noted, but they expected to arrive by dawn.

To the north, the last point of attack was on the eastern side of the ridge in Crow Creek Valley. "On the 9th we made a strong demonstration against the enemy's right," Schofield reported, "as a diversion in favor of operations upon his rear through Snake Creek Gap." Henry Judah's 2nd Division, XXIII Corps, formed 2 miles northeast of the ridge, facing south, with Cox's 3rd Division on their left. Confronting them were Stevenson's and Hindman's

Divisions of Hood's Corps, aligned across the valley and supported by artillery on a prominence known as Potato Hill. The Federal troops made some progress pushing the enemy back behind their main line, but no farther. Cox reported, "the works were found to be very strong, and the enemy was not tempted to leave them."

Things could not be going better for Johnston. Wheeler recommended making a circuit of the Federal army, similar to Stuart's ride around McClellan during the Peninsula Campaign, but Johnston felt it would take too much time and directed him to "push on to the rear of Tunnel Hill." He needed to know "whether the army of the enemy is west and on the Rocky Face, or to the north." Sherman's attempt to keep his foe in the dark about McPherson's destination appeared to be working.

The engagement at Snake Creek Gap. McPherson emerged on Johnston's flank virtually unopposed, as Sherman hoped, but was forced to use mounted infantry for reconnaissance because his cavalry had not yet arrived. (LOC)

At 5.00am on the 9th, McPherson's 24,000 men emerged from Snake Creek Gap. The 9th Illinois Mounted Infantry of Dodge's 2nd Brigade, 2nd Division, XVI Corps, encountered "the enemy's cavalry pickets on debouching from the gap." Grigsby's brigade had just arrived from its overnight ride from Dug Gap. Dodge had expected some resistance, but Grigsby was taken by surprise. "The 9th Illinois, which Grigsby took to be the Georgia troops he'd been told to expect," Breckenridge recounted, "were several hundred yards away and he sent a few of his scouts ahead to greet them. Suddenly a long skirmish-line broke from the woods. Behind the skirmish-line was developed a line of infantry." Grigsby made a fighting retreat towards Resaca.

Breckenridge later voiced his thoughts on Johnston's apparent lack of concern for Snake Creek Gap and Dug Gap. "That they were not guarded, and that this gave Sherman the easy means of causing the evacuation of Dalton and the retreat to Resaca, is undoubtedly true." There is no doubt that Johnston was more concerned about the enemy in his front than the possibility of one in his rear. William W. Mackall, Johnston's Chief of Staff, notified Wheeler of Johnston's desire for at least "some cavalry in observation between this place and Resaca for fear of a surprise," but added, "I do not think Resaca in any danger."

Fortunately for Johnston, Brigadier-General James Cantey's brigade had been sent from Rome to Resaca on the 5th. By the 9th, several thousand Confederate infantry, in Johnston's opinion more than enough to handle any contingency, were digging in on a hill west of the railroad and the Oostanaula River.

McPherson notified Sherman that he had encountered a brigade of cavalry but was unable to determine if there were "any considerable force of infantry at Resaca or not. Will know soon." The Federals inched forward until about 3 miles from the town, when the 9th Illinois encountered a "considerable infantry force."

Dodge was told to develop the enemy, "in line of battle or in his fortifications." His 2nd Division drove Cantey's 37th Mississippi back and occupied the prominence, called Bald Hill, a quarter of a mile away. McPherson rode up and directed Dodge to send "a few mounted men up the Dalton Road," to find an approach to the railroad in that direction. A small detachment of the 9th Illinois, 18 men in total, struck the railroad 2 miles south of Tilton, and cut the telegraph, but could not damage the railroad itself before they were chased off by enemy patrols.

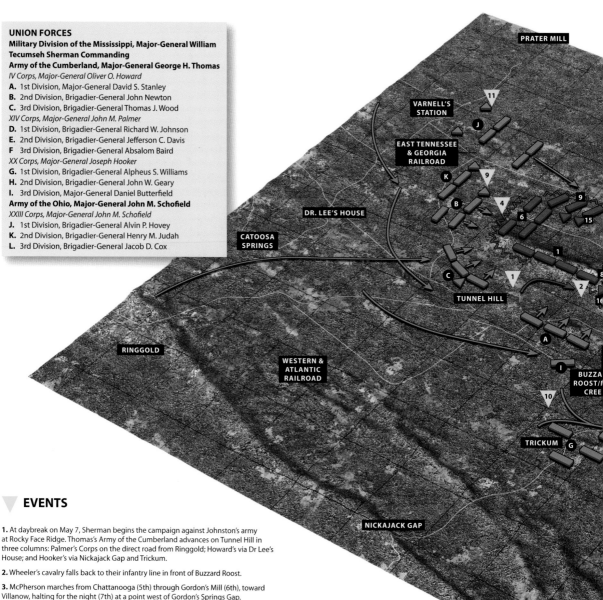

UNION FORCES

Military Division of the Mississippi, Major-General William Tecumseh Sherman Commanding

Army of the Cumberland, Major-General George H. Thomas

IV Corps, Major-General Oliver O. Howard
A. 1st Division, Major-General David S. Stanley
B. 2nd Division, Brigadier-General John Newton
C. 3rd Division, Brigadier-General Thomas J. Wood

XIV Corps, Major-General John M. Palmer
D. 1st Division, Brigadier-General Richard W. Johnson
E. 2nd Division, Brigadier-General Jefferson C. Davis
F 3rd Division, Brigadier-General Absalom Baird

XX Corps, Major-General Joseph Hooker
G. 1st Division, Brigadier-General Alpheus S. Williams
H. 2nd Division, Brigadier-General John W. Geary
I. 3rd Division, Major-General Daniel Butterfield

Army of the Ohio, Major-General John M. Schofield

XXIII Corps, Major-General John M. Schofield
J. 1st Division, Brigadier-General Alvin P. Hovey
K. 2nd Division, Brigadier-General Henry M. Judah
L. 3rd Division, Brigadier-General Jacob D. Cox

Map labels: PRATER MILL, VARNELL'S STATION, EAST TENNESSEE & GEORGIA RAILROAD, DR. LEE'S HOUSE, CATOOSA SPRINGS, TUNNEL HILL, RINGGOLD, WESTERN & ATLANTIC RAILROAD, BUZZARD ROOST/ CREE, TRICKUM, NICKAJACK GAP, GORDON' SPRING

▼ EVENTS

1. At daybreak on May 7, Sherman begins the campaign against Johnston's army at Rocky Face Ridge. Thomas's Army of the Cumberland advances on Tunnel Hill in three columns: Palmer's Corps on the direct road from Ringgold; Howard's via Dr Lee's House; and Hooker's via Nickajack Gap and Trickum.

2. Wheeler's cavalry falls back to their infantry line in front of Buzzard Roost.

3. McPherson marches from Chattanooga (5th) through Gordon's Mill (6th), toward Villanow, halting for the night (7th) at a point west of Gordon's Springs Gap.

4. May 8, Newton directs Harker's brigade, with Wagner on his left and Sherman in reserve, to push along the northern crest of Rocky Face Ridge. Severely constricted by the terrain and the rebel entrenchments, they are unable to advance more than a mile.

5. Wood's division (IV Corps), Davis (XIV Corps), and Butterfield (XX Corps) drive the enemy to his entrenchments along the western crest of Rocky Face Ridge, and occupy the mouth of Buzzard Roost, but are unable to drive him any farther.

6. Geary's division (XX Corps) moves south to Dug Gap where it encounters the 9th Kentucky Cavalry and the 1st and 2nd Arkansas infantry of Williamson's brigade and are unable to make any headway. Granbury's brigade of Cleburne's division fortifies the Rebel line after nightfall.

7. At 5.00am on the 9th, Dodge's Corps, followed closely by Logan's Corps, passes through Snake Creek Gap. Advancing toward Sherman's ultimate objective, the Western & Atlantic Railroad at Resaca, McPherson, not expecting any resistance, becomes apprehensive when he encounters a lone Rebel brigade supported by a single cavalry regiment. He directs his men to fall back to the mouth of the gap, entrench, and wait for orders from Sherman.

8. Johnston, responding to reports that McPherson is advancing on his far left through Snake Creek Gap, orders Cleburne and Walker south.

9. Schofield makes a strong demonstration against the enemy's right, across Crow Creek Valley east of Rocky Face Ridge, as a diversion. Judah's division is on the right, with his flank resting at the foot of the mountain, with Cox on the left and Hovey in reserve. The corps advances steadily, driving the enemy into their main works, but no farther. Stevenson's and Hindman's divisions are aligned across the valley with Rowan's Georgia Battery firing from Potato Hill. Schofield is forced to withdraw to his previous position

10. Disappointed that McPherson is unable to destroy the railroad at Resaca, Sherman directs Hooker to send Williams and Butterfield to McPherson's support on the 10th, and the next day a general movement of Union forces to Resaca begins.

11. By May 12, Schofield has moved through Villanow to Snake Creek Gap, leaving Howard, with Stoneman's cavalry, recently arrived from Cleveland, and McCook, as the only Union forces still in the vicinity of Rocky Face Ridge. Wheeler skirmishes with McCook at Prater Mill, trying to determine the position of the Federal troops.

12. At 1.00am on May 13, Johnston, concerned for his supply line, orders all Confederate troops to withdraw from their entrenchments around Rocky Face Ridge and march to Resaca. Howard occupies Dalton at 9.00am.

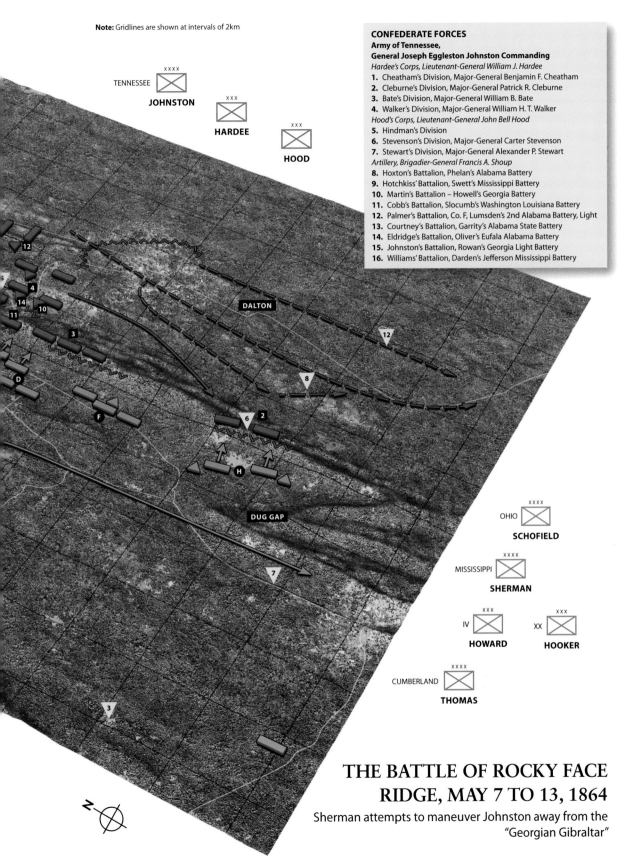

Note: Gridlines are shown at intervals of 2km

THE BATTLE OF ROCKY FACE RIDGE, MAY 7 TO 13, 1864

Sherman attempts to maneuver Johnston away from the "Georgian Gibraltar"

Major-General James Birdseye McPherson. "Such an opportunity does not occur twice in a single life," Sherman noted, of his subordinate's reluctance to "break the road," at Resaca. (LOC)

The battle of Resaca. James Cantey's 4,000-man brigade rushed to Resaca from Rome, Georgia, and dug in, managing to hold off McPherson's 24,000-man Army of the Tennessee from this position. (LOC)

Finally, at 4.00pm, Dodge was ordered to move on Resaca and the railroad. This was the key to Sherman's plan. Fuller's 1st Brigade crossed Camp Creek, but just as the skirmishers were in sight of the railroad, McPherson ordered Dodge to pull back and retire to Snake Creek Gap for the night.

McPherson explained that he believed he "could not succeed in cutting the railroad before dark," and decided to withdraw. He was becoming increasingly concerned about the exposure of his troops to enemy fire, and was still uncertain about the strength and deployment of the rebel infantry. His message to Sherman stated that the enemy, "displayed considerable force, and opened on us with artillery." He lost six men killed and 30 wounded.

Sherman showed remarkable self-constraint when he notified General Halleck in Washington of McPherson's failure. He told Halleck that "we will have to fight it out," and immediately set about modifying his original plan by moving Major-General George Stoneman's cavalry division into the area north of Rocky Face Ridge occupied by Schofield's infantry, and sending Thomas's and Schofield's armies through Snake Creek Gap to join McPherson.

Johnston and his subordinate commanders were having a hard time figuring out Sherman's intentions. Hardee told Wheeler, "I am unable to decide what the Yankees are endeavoring to accomplish. There seems to be no force threatening us except on Rocky Face, and that force has been unusually quiet to-day." When Johnston learned of Cantey's encounter with McPherson, he ordered Hood to Resaca with Hindman's, Cleburne's, and Walker's divisions, but when Cantey reported that the enemy seemed to be falling back, he changed his mind. He told Hood to leave Cleburne and Walker near Tilton, on the Resaca Road, and wait for developments.

On the 11th, Johnston told Bragg that the enemy, having failed at Rocky Face Ridge, was "making strong demonstrations on Resaca." The pace of operations began to pick up when Wheeler was notified that "General Hardee reports at 6 a.m., no enemy in Crow's Valley, none on his right, and is of opinion that they are moving by their right toward Oostanaula."

Johnston directed Polk, then at Rome, to go to Resaca at once. Shortly thereafter, Cantey reported, "Enemy advancing on this place in force." By early afternoon of the 12th, Johnston was convinced that the Federal army was "in motion for Calhoun or some place on the Oostanaula. I will follow this movement." Polk reached Resaca that afternoon.

By 1.00am on the 13th, Hood and Hardee were finally on their way south. The Confederate line extended north from the Oostanaula River for two and a half miles, following a series of wooded hills to an angle, then on a wide arc to the east, for another mile and a half, crossing the railroad and intersecting with the Connasauga River. Cantey occupied the extreme left. To his right was Polk, followed by Hardee, whose divisions extended to the angle. Hood's troops faced north across the Dalton road.

Sherman left Stoneman north of Dalton and Howard's Corps west of Rocky Face Ridge, while the rest of the grand army marched south. By the 13th, the Union forces were in place, paralleling Johnston's line from the Oostanaula River, along the west side of Camp Creek, then similarly arcing east to the railroad. Howard entered Dalton at 9.00am, reporting that "the railroad is entirely uninjured up to this point. I will make it a depot at once." The Federal supply line was secure and the Gibraltar of Georgia was behind them, along with 200 dead and another 637 wounded, but Sherman would soon learn that assaulting Resaca was no easier task.

THE BATTLE OF RESACA, MAY 14–15, 1864

Polk's 14,000 troops easily replaced the 600 casualties Johnston suffered defending the ridge. His new position was well covered with earthworks and rifle pits, built into high ridges not nearly as severe as Rocky Face Ridge but formidable enough. The artillery was emplaced with crossing fields of fire, especially where the line made its turn to the east.

The Federals were again hampered by the terrain. Country roads aided their maneuverability behind the line, but approaching the front itself, conditions deteriorated rapidly. According to Jacob Cox, whose division would be at the center of the assault on the 14th, "it required extraordinary exertions to take the artillery across the ravines and streams which had to be passed."

Early on the 14th, Sweeny's 2nd Division of Dodge's Corps was ordered to Lay's Ferry, 4 miles west of Resaca, "to secure a crossing of the Oostanaula." The 66th Illinois and 81st Ohio made the crossing and had just driven the Confederate pickets from their rifle pits, when it was reported that "the enemy was crossing in force at Calhoun Ferry," 2 miles upriver. Sweeny decided to withdraw his men until he could ascertain the truth of the rumor.

The fight of the day began on the north–south axis of the front, along Camp Creek. The plan, according to Brigadier-General Richard W. Johnson, commanding 1st Division, XIV Corps, called for a right wheel, "as a pivot through an arc of 130 degrees or thereabouts, or, at any rate, until the works and position of the enemy should be developed." With its right anchored on XX Corps north of Bald Hill, Carlin's 1st Brigade of Johnson's division stepped out at 9.00am, with elements of

Lay's Ferry. Sweeny's division of Dodge's Corps crossed the Oostanaula River, pulled back, and then crossed again a day later, setting off a chain of events that eventually forced the Confederate withdrawal from Resaca. (Author's collection)

From Resaca to the Etowah River, May 9 to 20, 1864

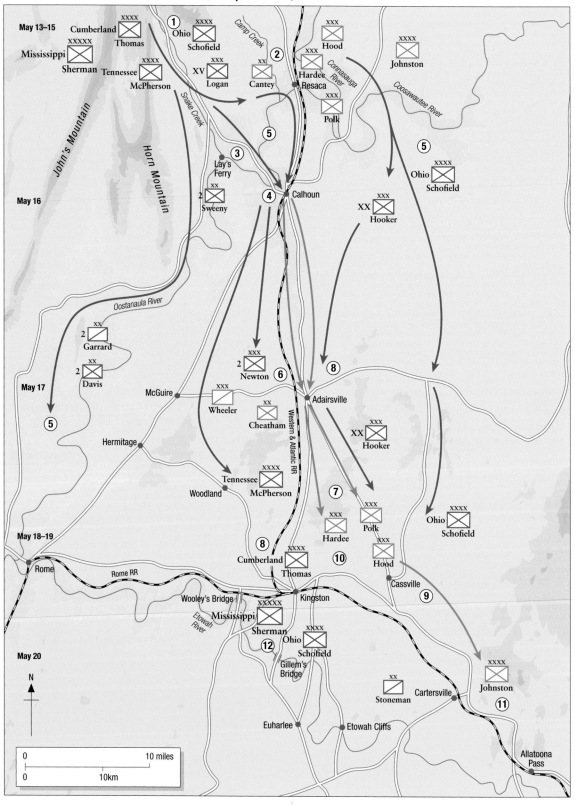

1. On May 9, as Thomas and Schofield hold Johnston at Rocky Face Ridge, McPherson, with Logan's corps in the lead, advances through Snake Creek Gap and engages Canty's Division west of Resaca. Thomas and Schofield follow on the 10th.
2. Belatedly acknowledging the threat to his flank, Johnston orders Hood and Hardee to move to Resaca on the 12th, to join Polk, recently arrived from Alabama. For three days, the two sides clash along Camp Creek, with neither side gaining an advantage.
3. On the 15th, Sweeny's Division of Dodge's Corps crosses the Oostanaula River at Lay's Ferry, posing a new threat to Johnston's flank and supply line.
4. Later that evening, Johnston orders a withdrawal to Calhoun.
5. Sherman pursues, sending Thomas, minus Hooker's corps, along the railroad, and Jeff Davis' infantry division of Palmer's corps, with Garrard's cavalry to Rome, while Schofield and Hooker cross on the left. McPherson crosses the river at Lay's Ferry
6. Johnston's three corps continue to Adairsville. There, on the 17th, Newton's division, the head of Thomas' column, skirmishes with Cheatham's division and Wheeler's cavalry, Johnston's rearguard.
7. On the 18th, Johnston tries to set a trap for Sherman's divided columns, sending Hardee to Kingston, north of the Etowah River, while Hood and Polk take the direct road to Cassville, seven miles east.
8. Sherman takes the bait, marching with Thomas towards Kingston, while McPherson moves four miles to the west at Woodland. Hooker follows the same road taken by Hood and Polk, while Schofield swings east.
9. Hood becomes alarmed at a report of Federal troops on his right flank and convinces Johnston to call off the attack. With Thomas now advancing from Kingston, Johnston pulls back to Cassville Cemetery on the south side of the town.
10. Thomas' artillery begins shelling the new Confederate line late on the 19th, as McPherson, Schofield, and Hooker close in.
11. Overnight, Hood and Polk become concerned that the Federal artillery will make their lines untenable, and convince Johnston to retreat across the Etowah River, which he does on the 20th.
12. Sherman decides not to pursue until his army can be resupplied and the railroad repaired. Thomas goes into camp at Cassville; McPherson at Kingston; and Schofield, with Stoneman's cavalry, patrolling between Cassville Depot, Cartersville, and the Etowah Bridge.

XXIII and IV Corps to their left. The advance was disjointed, "owing to the extremely rugged characteristic of the ground." Camp Creek and 400 yards of uneven ground separated them from the enemy.

Cleburne described the attack simply: "the enemy came into position on the ridge opposite to me, and opened a heavy fusillade. In the course of the afternoon he made several attempts to charge, but uniformly they were unhappy failures." Carlin's brigade was forced to take refuge along the eastern edge of the creek and when a battery of the 1st Ohio Light Artillery was brought up, the entire affair turned into a desultory artillery exchange. Carlin reported over 200 killed and wounded.

At the angle itself, Schofield's Corps met the same fate. Cox's division crossed the creek and secured a line of entrenchments in its front, "driving the enemy back upon a second line some 250 yards," but Judah's division on its right was caught in a murderous crossfire from its front and right, and "were repulsed with considerable loss." Cox's men held on to their advanced position, eventually running out of ammunition, until Newton's and Wood's divisions came to their support. Cox lost 61 killed and 476 wounded or missing. Walthall's brigade of Hood's Corps, which bore the brunt of Cox's attack along with Lewis's brigade of Hardee's Corps, lost 49 killed and 120 wounded or missing.

As Cox described the situation, "the movement of the morning had crowded our forces too much to the right, and Howard's left was in the air." Hooker's Corps was directed to move from the far right to the far left, a distance of nearly 4 miles across the same difficult ground that was wreaking such havoc on the Union attack. Late in the afternoon, Hood realized Howard's left was vulnerable and ordered a left wheel using Stewart's and Stevenson's divisions to turn the exposed flank and roll up the Union line.

The Confederates now experienced the same difficulties facing the Federals. Stewart's division, on the rim of the wheel, became totally disorganized, and the attack went off without it. Stevenson's brigades were initially successful in causing a wild Federal retreat, but Captain Peter Simonson's 5th Indiana Battery was so effective that the Rebels paused to make a bayonet attack on his six guns. Suddenly, from the woods, the 143rd New York Infantry, 82nd Illinois and 45th New York "moved rapidly down the steep ridge, at the same time wheeling to the right, charged over the barricades and met the advancing rebels, opening heavily upon them." It was Stevenson's men who were now falling back in confusion from the units of Hooker's Corps that had just completed their cross-battlefield march. Hood's attack was checked, at least for the day.

About mid-afternoon, a significant event occurred near the river. Major-General Peter J. Osterhaus, commanding Logan's 1st Division, was ordered to "make a demonstration along the whole line, opening with all the guns," for the purpose of preventing Polk from sending assistance to Hood or Hardee. At 5.30pm, the 76th Ohio, 27th Missouri, 30th Ohio, and 3rd Missouri, approximately 1,300 men, charged across Camp Creek and seized a hill that gave them a view of the town, the railroad, and the railroad bridge. They fought off a fierce counterattack, then, during the night, brought up their artillery, consisting of two 12-pdr howitzers, two 3in. ordnance rifles, two 20-pdr Parrotts, and four 12-pdr Napoleons. The position of these guns, less than 500 yards from the railroad, would have a critical impact on Johnston's decision-making over the next 24 hours.

Johnston was determined to exploit what he believed was a fatal flaw in the Federal line by ordering Hood to resume his attack on the right, early on the 15th. Soon, however, he learned that Howard's Corps had arrived from Dalton to strengthen the position Hood was expecting to attack. This was bad enough, but when he was informed of the threat McPherson's artillery now posed to his only open outlet to the south, he canceled Hood's orders. When he was told of Union troops crossing the Oostanaula, he knew he had made the right decision, and ordered Walker's division on a night march to confront Sweeny.

Sweeny's withdrawal, following the unfounded rumor that Confederate troops were threatening his flank, meant that when Walker arrived the next morning, he believed that the report of Federal troops on the south bank was also just a rumor, and reported it as such to Johnston. Johnston decided to give Hood the go-ahead to attack the Federal left flank, just as Sweeny was returning to Lay's Ferry. Sweeny's division recrossed the river and began throwing up earthworks, under the protection of two batteries of the First Missouri Light Artillery. By mid-afternoon, Hood was finally ready to go forward when he again received an order from Johnston, canceling the attack. Walker had notified Johnston that there really were Federal troops south of the Oostanaula.

That evening, Johnston directed the evacuation of Resaca. The railroad bridge burned in their wake. Sherman estimated Union casualties, "up to that time," at 600 killed and 3,375 wounded, with the two-day battle of Resaca accounting for 75 percent of those. Confederate casualties at Resaca were estimated at 2,800.

TO THE ETOWAH RIVER, MAY 16–20, 1864

At dawn on the 16th, Newton's skirmishers found the Confederate entrenchments abandoned. According to Sherman, "Johnston escaped, retreating south across the Oostanaula." The pursuit began, "General Thomas directly on his heels, General McPherson by Lay's Ferry, and General Schofield by obscure roads to the left."

Johnston "hoped to find a good defensive position near Calhoun," 5 miles from Resaca, but was unsuccessful, and finally stopped in a valley just north of Adairsville, 8 miles farther south. Cheatham and Wheeler skirmished with Newton's division while the army rested. Johnston decided the valley was too wide to defend properly, and moved on to Cassville, another 10 miles due south. On the way, he devised a trap for Sherman's army.

Two roads led south from Adairsville: one directly to Cassville, but away from the railroad, and the second following the rail line to Kingston, 6 miles to the west. "The probability that the Federal army would divide – a column following each road – gave me a hope of engaging and defeating one of them before it could receive aid from the other." On the 18th, Hardee's Corps, Wheeler's cavalry, and the army's trains followed the Kingston road, raising as much dust as possible, hoping to entice Sherman into believing that Johnston's army had gone that way. Polk and Hood marched directly to Cassville.

Sherman took the bait. McPherson and Thomas, minus XX Corps, followed Hardee to Kingston, while Hooker, followed by Schofield, proceeded in the direction of Cassville. Polk took up a position north of the town, ready to make a demonstration on Hooker's front in the morning. Hood, on his right, would then come in on Hooker's left flank. Destruction of the Union army would follow.

Unfortunately for Johnston, Brigadier-General Edward McCook's 1st Cavalry Division had been ordered to reconnoiter to the east on the morning of the 19th. It encountered Stevenson's division of Hood's Corps 4 miles from Cassville on the Canton road, in the rear of the Rebel line, and in a direction Hood believed was free of Yankees. McCook withdrew, but Hood, not knowing what else was out there, turned his corps about. By the time he was satisfied that his flank was safe, the sound of Federal artillery could be heard from the direction of Kingston. Johnston knew that the delay had allowed Sherman's main column to close on him. "The intention was therefore abandoned," he grudgingly decided, and his army withdrew to a line south of Cassville late in the day.

The new Confederate position was on a ridge below the town, directly behind the cemetery. Polk held the center, with Hardee on the left and Hood on the right, drawn up in two lines facing west. The town was hidden by trees, but "fresh-made parapets and the movements of men," could be seen on a range of hills beyond it, Sherman reported. "I ordered two field-batteries to close up at a gallop." While the artillery fired at long range, skirmishing was kept up all night as the troops prepared for a daylight attack. "When day broke the next morning, May 20th, the enemy was gone."

The evening before, Johnston's corps commanders had expressed their concerns about the Federal guns. Brigadier-General Francis Shoup, Johnston's Chief of Artillery, pointed out a section of Polk's line that might be enfiladed from

The Confederate Line at Cassville. Johnston called the second Confederate position at Cassville, on a ridge behind the cemetery, "the best I saw occupied during the war." (Author's collection)

THE FIGHT FOR THE FOUR-GUN BATTERY, RESACA, MAY 15, 1864 (PP. 42–43)

On May 13, after realizing that he had been flanked at Rocky Face Ridge, Confederate General Joseph Johnston withdrew to the hills around Resaca. For four days, Union troops had been building up, preparing to make a push for the Western & Atlantic Railroad, Johnston's main supply line. Full-scale fighting began on the 14th, with Union troops unable to make any advance except on the Rebel right flank, where Sherman failed to follow up his advantage. May 15 dawned with both sides intending to attack on the north end of the battlefield. General Oliver O. Howard's Union IV Corps went in first, at 1.00pm, assaulting Confederate General Thomas Hindman's division. When the lead Union brigade lost 120 men in 30 seconds, its commander, General William Hazen, ordered them back into their fortifications. Howard's initial attack failed in spite of a massive barrage by Federal artillery to soften up the Confederate position. In an attempt to offer some relief to Hindman's men with counter-battery fire, Confederate General John Bell Hood ordered Captain Max Van Den Corput's artillery battery forward, in advance of the Southern lines.

Corput's "Cherokee Artillery" was placed in position about 80 yards in front of the main Confederate line and protected by an earthen parapet. It was hardly in position when Union troops attacked again. The attack occurred so quickly that the Confederate artillerists were forced to abandon their guns.

Supporting fire from Rebel infantry kept the assaulting Federals pinned down, and the artillery pieces, four 12-pdr Napoleons, became trapped in a no man's land. According to a witness at the scene, "It was impossible to remove the artillery before the enemy had effected a lodgment in the ravine in front of it, thus placing it in such a position that while the enemy were entirely unable to remove it, we were equally so, without driving off the enemy massed in the ravine beyond it, which would have been attended with great loss of life." Over the course of the afternoon, the Federals sent three different brigades into the breach in an attempt to capture the rebel battery.

The most determined of those attacks was the charge of the 70th Indiana, under the command of future US President, Colonel Benjamin Harrison. The artwork shows (1) Harrison, on horseback, with saber in hand, leading the charge as the (2) Indianans swarm over the parapet and overwhelm the (3) gunners in hand-to-hand fighting. From the top of the hill and on both flanks, Tennessee regiments of Brown's brigade of (4) Stevenson's division poured volley after volley into the attackers, forcing them back over the embankment to take shelter on the downhill side. "Come on and take those guns!" taunted Brown's Tennesseans. "Come and take 'em yourselves!" the Federals yelled back. It was only after nightfall that a breach was made in the embankment and the guns were dragged away to the Union lines.

the hill beyond the rebel right. "General Polk, if attacked, cannot hold his position three quarters of an hour," Hood exclaimed, "and I cannot hold mine two hours." Johnston "yielded at last," to his two lieutenants. During the night, the army crossed the Etowah River and went into camp around Allatoona Mountain, 4 miles to the south.

THE BATTLES AROUND NEW HOPE CHURCH, MAY 21 TO JUNE 10

In less than two weeks, Johnston had given up 50 miles of northwest Georgia and was nearly closer to Atlanta than he had been to Chattanooga on the 7th. He reassured Richmond that, despite the retrograde movement, Sherman's supply lines were getting longer while his were getting shorter. His losses had been minimal so far, 3,388 killed and wounded, not including cavalry, so that his army had actually increased in combat manpower with the addition of troops previously assigned to guard his shortening supply line. Perhaps most importantly, he had kept Sherman from detaching troops to reinforce Grant, who was suffering horrendous losses in Virginia. Bragg replied that, "from the high condition in which your army is reported, we confidently rely on a brilliant success."

Johnston liked his army's position near Allatoona. What he did not know was that Sherman "knew more of Georgia than the rebels did." Twenty years earlier, the Federal commander had traversed this same region as a lieutenant of the Third Artillery at Marietta. Sherman gave his army a three-day rest while the railroad was repaired to Kingston. On May 23, with 20 days' rations in the wagons, the three Federal armies set off cross-country on a wide swing to the south, passing no closer than 8 miles to Johnston's position. Their objective was the Confederate supply depot at Marietta, 15 miles southeast of Allatoona. They would converge in the vicinity of Dallas, roughly 20 miles as the crow flies from their camps along the Etowah River.

"The country here is very desolate," wrote a correspondent for the *Mobile Daily Advertiser and Register*, "not a house more attractive than a miserable cabin can be seen. The population, like the soil, is poor and disaffected. Most of the men are off in the woods, and the women are silent, ignorant, and surly. It is the midnight corner of Georgia." To the soldiers who fought there for both sides, it would soon be known as the "Hell-Hole."

Jackson's cavalry reported Union troops crossing the river south of Kingston on the 23rd. Johnston reacted quickly. Hardee marched that afternoon to the small crossroads at New Hope Church, with Hood following the next day. Polk traveled on a parallel route a little farther to the east and, by the 25th, all three corps were in line facing west, in heavily wooded country, awaiting the unsuspecting Federals.

Anthony Cooper's Furnace. All that remains of the once-thriving ironworks on the Etowah River that supplied iron for the Western & Atlantic Railroad, 5 miles west. It was destroyed by Union troops during the campaign. (Author's collection)

Operations around New Hope Church, May 21 to June 5, 1864

1. Following their crossing of the Etowah River, Johnston's army is encamped near the Western & Atlantic Railroad at Allatoona Pass.
2. On May 23, Sherman orders a cross-country advance towards Dallas for the purpose of flanking Johnston out of his stronghold at Allatoona Pass and seizing the Confederate supply depot at Marietta. Thomas occupies the Federal center, following the Stilesboro Road through Euharlee, with McPherson on his right. Schofield marches on Thomas' left flank, and is observed by Jackson's cavalry
3. That afternoon, Jackson notifies Johnston of the Federal advance. Johnston directs Hardee, with Polk on his left, to march through New Hope Church to Dallas. Hood follows Hardee's route on the 24th.
4. Wheeler attacks a Union supply train near Cassville on the 24th, and confirms that the Federal army is on the move to the south.
5. On the afternoon of May 25, Hooker, with Geary in the lead, encounters Stewart's division of Hood's corps dug in at New Hope Church. Hooker fails to make any headway and is forced to fall back and entrench. The battle is renewed the next day, with no advantage to either side.

6. On the 26th, McPherson arrives in Dallas and deploys east of the town, with Davis' division of XIV Corps on his left.
7. On the 27th, Sherman sends Howard toward Pickett's Mill in an attempt to get around Johnston's right flank. Struggling through thick woods and rugged terrain, Wood's division, with Hazen in the lead, is violently repulsed by Cleburne's division.
8. Johnston, believing that Sherman's right flank is vulnerable, sends Hardee, with Bate's division in the lead, against the Federal line at Dallas. Logan and Dodge successfully fend off the Rebel attack.
9. Over the next week, skirmishing continues as both sides entrench along a 7-mile front. Sherman abandons his idea of reaching Marietta and extends his line around Johnston's right in an attempt to get back to the railroad at Acworth.
10. On June 1, Sherman orders Stoneman's and Garrard's cavalry divisions to the east and west ends, respectively, of Johnston's now abandoned position at Allatoona Pass.
11. On June 4, realizing he cannot keep pace with Sherman's flanking maneuver, Johnston orders a general withdrawal to a new line running from Lost Mountain on the Dallas–Marietta Road, northeast through Pine Mountain to Brush Mountain.
12. The same day, Sherman directs a concentration of his armies around Acworth awaiting repair of the railroad, reinforcement, and resupply.

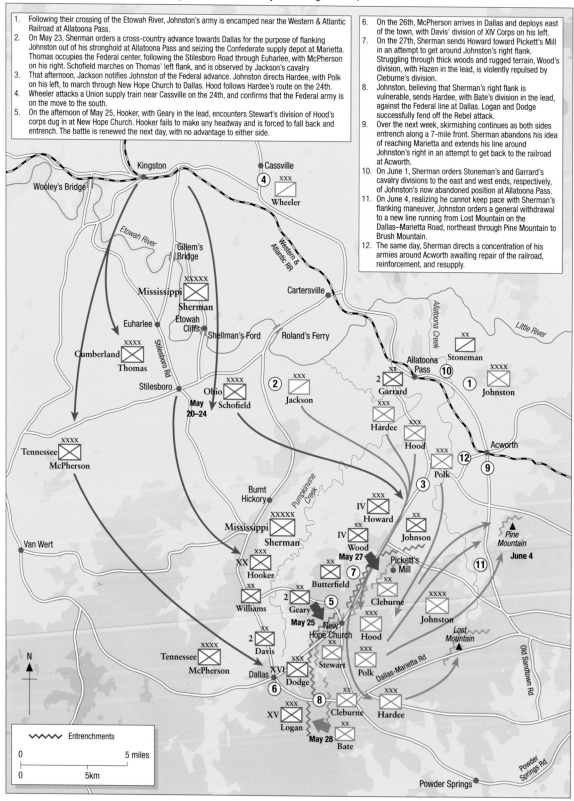

At 7.00am on the 25th, Geary's division marched toward New Hope Church, with Williams' and Butterfield's divisions following secondary roads to the right and left. The rest of Thomas's army was 5 miles back. A group of Federal cavalrymen captured a Confederate courier carrying a dispatch for General Jackson, informing him that Johnston's army was headed his way. Sherman dismissed the message as nonsense.

By afternoon, Geary's three brigades, under Candy, Buschbeck, and Cobham, were advancing into thickening woods. Up ahead, the Federal skirmishers suddenly found themselves in a firefight with what appeared to be a substantial body of troops. Hood had dispatched Colonel Bushrod Jones and the 32nd and 58th Alabama, along with Austin's Louisiana Sharpshooters, 300 men in all, to "develop the enemy." Jones's small contingent put up a stiff resistance, before retiring, at a cost of 61 killed, wounded, and missing.

Geary extended his skirmish line to over a mile, and again pressed forward. Captured prisoners revealed that both Hood and Hardee were in their front. Geary and Hooker were concerned enough to request a temporary halt to enable Williams and Butterfield to close up the advance. Sherman concurred.

By 5.00pm, Hooker's additional divisions had arrived and immediately formed "for attack in columns by brigades," hoping to drive a wedge through the rebel line. They totaled more than 16,000 men. "The discharges of canister and shell from the enemy were heavier than in any other battle of the campaign in which my command were engaged," Geary reported. They soon found out they were attacking A. P. Stewart's division, the center of Hood's line. Charge after charge was made, while the man known as "Old Straight" rode back and forth, encouraging his men. "No more persistent attack or determined resistance was anywhere made," Stewart reported. When Johnston rode up and asked him if he needed assistance, the former mathematics professor replied, "My own troops will hold the position."

Allatoona Pass. Sherman had toured this area as a lieutenant in 1842. "I therefore knew that the Allatoona Pass was very strong, would be hard to force, and resolved not even to attempt to turn the position." (LOC)

The battle of New Hope Church. According to Sherman, New Hope Church was "the accidental intersection of the road leading from Allatoona to Dallas with that from Van Wert to Marietta." (LOC)

"The Hell Hole." Sergeant Rice Bull, of the 123rd New York, recorded that "the air was filled with the fumes of burning powder … the shot and shell from the enemy batteries tearing through the trees caused every head to duck." (LOC)

The attackers could get no closer than 50 yards. Then, sometime after 7.00pm, a furious thunderstorm erupted over the battlefield. "The rain came down in torrents," one Union sergeant recalled, "the lightening was blinding; then the darkness so black it could almost be felt." All across the line, men on both sides were running out of ammunition, and the fighting simply stopped. Hooker's Corps staggered away while Stewart's men cheered, just as Howard's Corps came on the scene, too late to join the fight. Preliminary estimates of Union casualties numbered 1,665. Stewart counted his losses at between three and four hundred. Both estimates were on the low side.

Dawn revealed "a strong line of intrenchments [sic] facing us, with a heavy force of infantry and guns. The battle was renewed," Sherman wrote, "but without success." Johnston, believing that Sherman would try to get to the railroad by going around the rebel right flank, moved Cleburne's division 5 miles to the northeast, from the vicinity of Dallas, which McPherson was now investing, to a place known as Pickett's Mill.

Around New Hope Church, each side occupied heavily wooded ridge lines 80 to 300 yards apart, and earthworks extended for over 5 miles. Skirmishers battled in the intervening no man's land, with neither side able to gain any advantage whatsoever, while sharpshooters prevented artillerymen from firing more than the occasional shot. It was a prelude to the Western Front of World War I. Late in the day, Hood noted that "the enemy were found to be extending their left," and sent Hindman's division around to his right, adjoining Cleburne.

As Johnston predicted, Sherman decided to try and turn the Confederate right 2 miles north of New Hope Church, on the 27th. Howard's Corps was selected for the honor. Wood's division held the center, in a column six lines deep, with Johnson on the left, and McLean's 1st Brigade, 2nd Division, XXIII Corps, on the right. Twice, they selected a point of attack only to discover enemy entrenchments in their front, each time pulling back and sidling farther to their left. Finally, about 5.00pm, they were ready to make their third attempt. "We still found a line of works to our right," Howard wrote, "but they did not seem to cover General Wood's front, and they were new, the enemy still working hard upon them."

Unbeknownst to Wood, he was coming in on the center of Cleburne's division, whose hastily built line extended a mile in either direction, not only covering Wood's front, but Johnson's and McLean's, as well. Wood told Howard, "We will put in Hazen and see what success he has." It did not take long. Colonel Benjamin F. Scribner, commanding Johnson's advance on the far left, came under fire from two dismounted brigades, numbering about 1,000 troopers of Brigadier-General John Kelly's cavalry division. Scribner halted and turned his men to face this threat to his flank thus exposing Hazen's left to the enemy. Conditions on Hazen's right compounded the problem.

"By some mistake of orders," Howard reported, "McLean's troops," directed to keep the rebel left busy, "did not show themselves to the enemy, nor open any fire to attract his attention." This failure allowed the combined 8th and 19th Arkansas regiments of Govan's brigade to shift from the left to the point of attack on the right. Hazen's brigade, numbering some 1,500, went in virtually unsupported. "The uproar was deafening; the air sibilant with streams and sheets of missiles," wrote author Ambrose Bierce, then a topographical engineer on Hazen's staff. Hazen was caught in a brutal crossfire. "Of the hundreds of corpses within twenty paces of the Confederate line, I venture to say that a third were within fifteen paces, and not one within ten." Hazen was shattered and fell back. Wood tried twice more, with Gibson's and Knefler's brigades, but neither could get closer than 100 yards to the Confederate line. "Under these circumstances it soon became evident that the assault had failed," Howard reported. Over 1,500 Union casualties littered the field, including over 500 dead or missing. Johnson was severely injured by a shell fragment. Cleburne numbered his losses at 85 killed, 363 wounded, plus an estimated 200 more from Kelly's division, out of 4,683 engaged.

The battle of Pickett's Mill. Hazen's brigade had to cross a deep ravine through thick underbrush, before emerging from the dense woods into an open field in front of Brigadier-General Hiram Granbury's Texas Brigade. (Author's collection)

Both Federal attacks, New Hope Church on the 25th and Pickett's Mill on the 27th, had been made by columns of brigades. As Cox noted in his report, "the result in both cases demonstrated that in a difficult and wooded country, and especially against intrenched lines, the column had little, if any advantage over a single line of equal front." Its depth, which should have provided momentum to the attacking force, actually "exposed masses of men to fire who were unable to fire in return." Then there were the fieldworks. "It is within bounds to say," Cox concluded, "that such works as were constantly built by the contending forces in Georgia made one man in the trench fully equal to three or four in the assault."

Johnston notified Bragg of his army's successes in the two battles, ending with the cautionary statement that the Federal army was still approaching the railroad, "at the rate of about a mile a day." He was convinced, however, that Pickett's Mill had exposed a vulnerability on Sherman's left flank, and directed Hood to make a night march of over 6 miles, to attack at daylight on the 28th.

Sherman realized that continuing to assault the entire Confederate army behind fortified lines was fruitless. He already controlled the road to Allatoona. Additionally, Major-General Blair was at Rome with the 15,000 men of XVII

Fieldworks. Sherman noted that "the parapets varied from four to six feet high, surmounted by a head-log resting in notches cut in other trunks which extended back, forming an inclined plane, in case the head-log should be knocked inward by a cannon-shot." (Author's collection)

Corps, waiting for the order to move to the front, and Stoneman's Cavalry was approaching Allatoona Pass. He determined to do precisely what Johnston predicted he would: push around the Confederate right to gain control of the Acworth Road and access, once again, to the railroad. First, he needed to pull McPherson from the right flank at Dallas and shift him to the left.

Hood arrived on the Federal left at dawn, only to discover that the Union line had been pulled back to a more defensible position and was solidly entrenched. Johnston told him to return to his starting point. If Sherman was strengthening his left, he must be pulling troops from his right, Johnston decided, and directed Hardee to probe the Union line at Dallas. "Fighting Billy" Bate's division was selected for this task. Bate's men, who had been in position for several days, knew that the Federal line was still well manned, but Bate persisted. McPherson had indeed received the directive from Sherman to begin moving to the north, but had barely begun to do so when the Confederate assault began.

At 3.45pm, on the 28th, Brigadier-General Frank Armstrong and his brigade of dismounted cavalry were ordered "to ascertain, by a forced reconnaissance, if those intrenchments were still held by adequate forces." He soon learned that they were. Logan's corps was formed with Harrow's division on the right, Morgan Smith's in the center, and Osterhaus's on the left. Bate's three brigades under Thomas Smith, Jesse Finley, and Joseph Lewis were in three separate columns, waiting for a signal from Armstrong to advance. One of the units Armstrong's men encountered was Colonel John Wilder's 3rd Brigade of dismounted cavalry from Garrard's division. It was armed with Spencer repeating rifles capable of firing up to 20 rounds per minute, compared with the usual three fired by the muzzle-loaders. "Armstrong was received with a cannonade and fire of musketry so spirited

Kennesaw Mountain from Big Shanty. Sherman knew the inherent strength of Johnston's newest line. "Kenesaw [*sic*] Mountain was his salient; his two flanks were refused and covered by parapets." (LOC)

that each of the brigade commanders supposed that all of the troops but his own were engaged, and ordered the assault of the works." Bate balked, sending couriers to his brigade commanders directing each to pull back, but only Smith received the order.

The attack faltered, and the results were similar to the previous three days' battles, but in reverse. Johnston noted his losses, somewhat matter-of-factly, as "three hundred men killed and wounded." Logan reported that "he buried over 300 of the enemy in his front and took 97 prisoners," estimating Confederate casualties at closer to 2,000 compared with 379 of his own.

The fighting around New Hope Church had successfully pulled Johnston from his strong position in Allatoona Pass, but Sherman had been thwarted in his attempt to get to Marietta. He reported to Halleck that Blair was near Rome and would be ordered to "march straight for Allatoona, which I infer the enemy has abandoned altogether. I will move to the left and resume railroad communications to the rear."

Sherman continued his eastward sidle on June 1 while Stoneman's cavalry seized the Allatoona Pass. Proceeding to Acworth, Stoneman entered the town, 4 miles south of Allatoona, on the 3rd, and reported, "the railroad and telegraph wire are both complete as far as Acworth, except the Etowah railroad bridge, and the country in our rear is entirely clear of the enemy."

Johnston was forced to pull back to the vicinity of Gilgal Church, 8 miles to the southeast, and halfway to Marietta. Hardee occupied the left of an 8-mile line, anchored on the 300-foot-high Lost Mountain, just north of the Dallas–Marietta Road, with Jackson's cavalry in support. Polk held the center around the equally high Pine Mountain, with the ever-vital railroad on his right. Hood's corps covered the far right, ending around another low hill called Brush Mountain, with Wheeler's cavalry on his flank. Three major roads, and the railroad, ran from the direction of Acworth. Three miles to the southeast was the highest peak in northwest Georgia, the 800-foot-high Kennesaw Mountain. Johnston, once again, had chosen well.

Sherman consolidated his three armies at Acworth and waited for the railroad bridge over the Etowah River to be repaired. Heavy rains turned everything to mud, but, by the 10th, the track was in order. Blair arrived, joining Logan and Dodge on the Federal left, and the advance resumed. Thomas was in his accustomed spot in the center with Schofield on the right. Garrard and Stoneman guarded the flanks. With Blair's corps joining the Army of the Tennessee, Sherman's numbers were now slightly higher than they had been at the beginning of May: 112,819 versus 110,123 of all arms. Johnston reported an effective strength of 79,809 on the returns for June 10.

THE BATTLES AROUND KENNESAW MOUNTAIN, JUNE 10 TO JULY 6

Hoping that Johnston had crossed the Chattahoochee, Sherman was frustrated to find that "another prolonged contest must be had around the commanding spurs of the mountains that covered Marietta." Hardee was concerned about Bate's position in a salient on his right, near Pine Mountain, and asked Johnston to ride out with him and determine whether it was vulnerable to envelopment. Polk joined them, and soon the three were standing on top of the mountain overlooking the encroaching Federal lines 300 feet below.

Sherman was conferring with Howard not far from Pine Mountain, when "I noticed a rebel battery on its crest," as well as "a group of the enemy, evidently observing us with glasses." He estimated the distance to the Confederate guns at about half a mile and directed a battery close by to fire off three rounds at the cluster of men on the hill. Johnston noticed the activity around the Federal artillery and cautioned everyone to scatter, which they did, except for Polk, who was struck by the second shell and killed instantly.

Sherman had ridden off before the guns even fired, and was unaware who had been on top of the hill. It was only later, when he stopped at a signal station and learned from one of the officers who had decoded a Confederate message that read, "Send an ambulance for General Polk's body," that he suspected what had happened. The next day, Union pickets found Pine Mountain abandoned, and a note stuck on a ramrod, "You damned Yankee sons of bitches have killed our old Genl. Polk."

Johnston was being pressed hard, and, on the 16th, contracted his lines by pulling his left flank back, swinging 90 degrees to the east, across Mud Creek. Two days later, his army went into prepared positions along Kennesaw Mountain. Polk's Corps, now under Major-General William W. Loring, held the slopes on a strong 3-mile segment confronting McPherson, with Hood on the right. To the south, across the Dallas road, Hardee placed Cleburne and Cheatham to face Thomas. The Federal advance slogged on through the wet weather. On the 21st, Sherman recorded in his notebook, "This is the nineteenth day of rain, and the prospect of fair weather is as far off as ever."

Sherman again looked for a way around Johnston's position. Hooker, on the right, was directed to advance toward Marietta, with Schofield on his right following the Powder Springs–Marietta Road. "Act according to circumstances," Sherman told Schofield, hoping that Johnston would once more try to slip away.

The Confederate commander was in no hurry to comply with Sherman's wishes, but he was concerned about his left flank. On the night of the 21st, he ordered Hood to pull back from the Confederate right, cross behind

The death of Polk. General Polk, who was dignified and corpulent, walked back slowly, not wishing to appear too hurried or cautious in the presence of his men, and was struck across the chest by an unexploded shell, which killed him instantly. (LOC)

From Kennesaw Mountain to the Chattahoochee River, June 6 to July 9, 1864

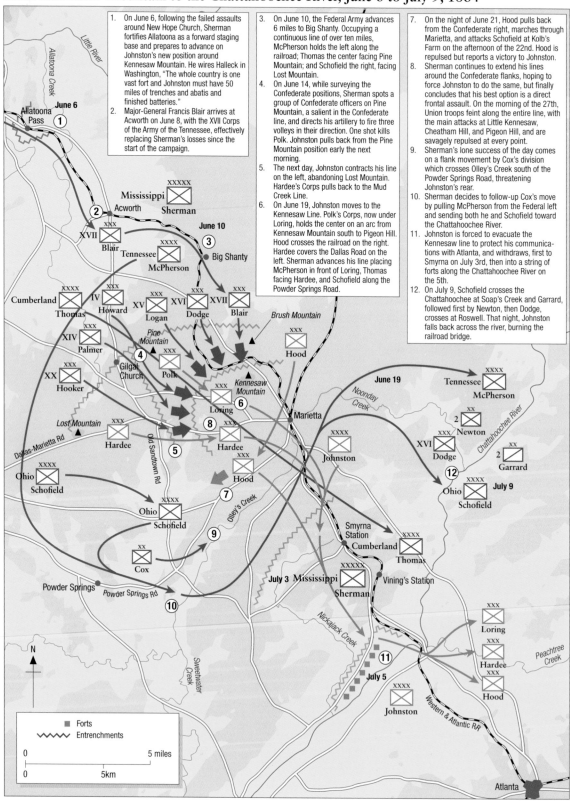

1. On June 6, following the failed assaults around New Hope Church, Sherman fortifies Allatoona as a forward staging base and prepares to advance on Johnston's new position around Kennesaw Mountain. He wires Halleck in Washington, "The whole country is one vast fort and Johnston must have 50 miles of trenches and abatis and finished batteries."
2. Major-General Francis Blair arrives at Acworth on June 8, with the XVII Corps of the Army of the Tennessee, effectively replacing Sherman's losses since the start of the campaign.
3. On June 10, the Federal Army advances 6 miles to Big Shanty. Occupying a continuous line of over ten miles, McPherson holds the left along the railroad; Thomas the center facing Pine Mountain; and Schofield the right, facing Lost Mountain.
4. On June 14, while surveying the Confederate positions, Sherman spots a group of Confederate officers on Pine Mountain, a salient in the Confederate line, and directs his artillery to fire three volleys in their direction. One shot kills Polk. Johnston pulls back from the Pine Mountain position early the next morning.
5. The next day, Johnston contracts his line on the left, abandoning Lost Mountain. Hardee's Corps pulls back to the Mud Creek Line.
6. On June 19, Johnston moves to the Kennesaw Line. Polk's Corps, now under Loring, holds the center on an arc from Kennesaw Mountain south to Pigeon Hill. Hood crosses the railroad on the right. Hardee covers the Dallas Road on the left. Sherman advances his line placing McPherson in front of Loring, Thomas facing Hardee, and the Powder Springs Road.
7. On the night of June 21, Hood pulls back from the Confederate right, marches through Marietta, and attacks Schofield at Kolb's Farm on the afternoon of the 22nd. Hood is repulsed but reports a victory to Johnston.
8. Sherman continues to extend his lines around the Confederate flanks, hoping to force Johnston to do the same, but finally concludes that his best option is a direct frontal assault. On the morning of the 27th, Union troops attack along the entire line, with the main attacks at Little Kennesaw, Cheatham Hill, and Pigeon Hill, and are savagely repulsed at every point.
9. Sherman's lone success of the day comes on a flank movement by Cox's division which crosses Olley's Creek south of the Powder Springs Road, threatening Johnston's rear.
10. Sherman decides to follow-up Cox's move by pulling McPherson from the Federal left and sending both he and Schofield toward the Chattahoochee River.
11. Johnston is forced to evacuate the Kennesaw line to protect his communications with Atlanta, and withdraws, first to Smyrna on July 3rd, then into a string of forts along the Chattahoochee River on the 5th.
12. On July 9, Schofield crosses the Chattahoochee at Soap's Creek and Garrard, followed first by Newton, then Dodge, crosses at Roswell. That night, Johnston falls back across the river, burning the railroad bridge.

the mountain, and slip into a new position to the left of Hardee. Loring and Wheeler covered Hood's vacated sector.

On the morning of the 22nd, Hascall's division of Schofield's Corps, numbering about 6,000 men, crossed Noyes Creek, on Hooker's right, and advanced towards the northeast. Cox's division, with 7,000 men, covered their right. By late morning, the Federals had reached Kolb's Farm, south of the Powder Springs Road, and had begun to throw up breastworks.

Early in the afternoon, the 123rd New York of Knipe's brigade of Hooker's Corps, and the 14th Kentucky of Silas Strickland's brigade of Hascall's division, went forward in a reconnaissance-in-force to find the enemy. Crossing an open field about 300 yards east of the farm, they encountered a strong skirmish line, which they drove through a belt of trees. Emerging from the woods, they halted to report the Rebel line half a mile ahead.

After pausing in Marietta overnight to give his men a brief rest, Hood advanced 4 miles down the Powder Springs Road, moving into line on Hardee's left. By 2.30pm, Stevenson had pushed out his skirmish line, while the remainder of the corps began to dig in. The Rebel skirmishers quickly ran into the 123rd New York and 14th Kentucky.

Hood apparently convinced himself that the two Union regiments were the prelude to an all-out attack, and, without assessing either the deployment of the enemy or the condition of the terrain, deployed for an attack of his own. Confederate prisoners captured in the earlier skirmishing reported that both Hood and Hardee were getting ready to advance, and Hooker ordered Williams and Geary, north of the Powder Springs Road, to prepare breastworks, while Schofield told Hascall, south of the road, to do the same. Five Federal batteries anchored the line.

Artillery had a greater effect on the outcome at Kennesaw Mountain than in any other battle in the campaign. At Kolb's Farm, Hood's attack was decimated by well-placed Federal guns. (Author's collection)

Hood was ready at 5.00pm, and the attackers quickly realized how little they knew of the situation in their front. Stevenson's division, forming the left wing, quickly discovered that it was impossible to keep any semblance of order to the lines. "The nature of the ground over which we passed was most unfavorable to such a movement," Stevenson reported, "the two right brigades moved for much of the way over open fields, the two left through dense undergrowth."

Those two left brigades, Brown's Tennessee and Cumming's Georgia, first encountered the stubborn 14th Kentucky, who pulled back, enabling the guns of Shield's and Paddock's batteries to open on the attackers. According to Cox, the canister from the guns, "with the fire from the breastworks, soon cleared the front." Stevenson paid particular tribute to the defenders, noting that the Federal artillery, "which was massed in large force and admirably posted, was served with a rapidity and fatal precision which could not be surpassed." Stevenson alone lost 870 men, more than a third of all his losses from May 7 to July 20.

Hindman's Division, forming the right wing, diverged from Stevenson's around a swampy ravine and got caught between Geary and Williams. "From the hill on Geary's right the 13th New York Artillery opened a rapid fire on the charging lines," Cox recounted. Canister and case from the guns, and a few volleys of musket fire was enough. "The repulse of the Confederates was complete."

Johnston admitted a loss of "about a thousand," but was perhaps more concerned that Hood had gone in without notifying him. At the time, Hood

The Confederate Line at Kennesaw Mountain. Kennesaw commands the area around it, and is visible from Atlanta on a clear day. Sherman was getting frustrated at the pace of operations. (LOC)

reported the battle as a victory in his favor, translating the Federal skirmish line into a full-scale attack that was "not only repulsed," but resulted in his divisions driving the enemy from their entrenchments. Unfortunately, "being exposed, in this position, to a fire of intrenched artillery, they had been compelled to withdraw." Years later, Johnston learned what had actually occurred.

Sherman was also having issues with one of his senior commanders. He could hear the Federal guns, but was unaware that a battle was raging on his right flank. Late in the evening, he received a message from Hooker, stating, "We have repulsed two heavy attacks and feel confident, our only apprehension being from our extreme right flank. Three corps are in front of us." Sherman knew for a fact, having ridden the line himself that afternoon, that Hooker was not facing three Confederate corps. Nor should his right be in danger, as Schofield was firmly on Hooker's flank. A later message from Schofield painted a more accurate picture of events, and Thomas reassured Sherman that he was confident that Hooker could not possibly be facing all three Confederate corps.

Sherman rode south through Butterfield's division and was bothered to find that they had not even been engaged in the action. Farther on, Geary and Williams were burying their dead. He met Hooker and Schofield along the Powder Springs Road, and showed the latter the dispatch he had received implying that Schofield was not covering Hooker's flank. Schofield "was very angry, and pretty sharp words passed" between him and Hooker. Hooker acted as if he was unaware of Schofield's deployment of Hascall the day before. Sherman told him, "Such a thing must not occur again." He felt that he had actually reproved Hooker "more gently than the occasion demanded," but "from that time he [Hooker] began to sulk."

Union Artillery. Cox noted the splendid performance of the 13th New York Artillery at Kolb's Farm: "Winegar's battery of three-inch rifles, and Woodbury's of light twelves joined in the cannonade." (LOC)

THE DEAD ANGLE, KENNESAW MOUNTAIN, JUNE 27, 1864 (PP. 58–59)

The end of June found Johnston's army strongly dug in along a 12-mile front centered on Kennesaw Mountain, a formidable peak some 20 miles northwest of Atlanta. Johnston's strategy of giving up ground in an attempt to stretch Sherman's supply line was finally having an effect on the Union commander. Sherman's frustration got the better of him, and he made plans to assault Johnston's entrenched troops.

On June 27, believing that Johnston's front must be stretched thin, Sherman planned to launch three probing attacks to find a weakness in the Rebel line. General McPherson, on the Union left, would lead his attack at a point near the southwest end of Kennesaw Ridge while General Schofield, on the Union right, was ordered to attack near the Powder Springs Road. General Thomas advanced in the center along the Dallas–Marietta Road, and that is where the hottest action of the day occurred. At the point where the divisions of Confederate generals Cleburne and Cheatham met, a hill formed a salient in the Confederate line. This ridge line soon came to be known by soldiers on both sides as "The Dead Angle."

The scene shows eight Union regiments, attacking mid-morning, crossing two open fields separated by a small swampy stream **(1)**. Five hundred yards away, at the top of a steep, rocky hill, the entrenched men of the 1st and 27th Tennessee regiments of Maney's brigade wait **(2)**. A row of Union cannons begins firing from the edge of the woods over the heads of the attacking Union troops. The attack on the left, up a steep incline covered with waist-high rows of tangled timber, falters near the top, and dead and wounded Union soldiers dot the hillside **(3)** as others try to make their escape. On the right, troops of the Union's 52nd Ohio lunge toward the base of the Rebel parapet atop a steep rise, amidst blinding smoke and sweltering heat. It was "a perfect pandemonium." In less than a half-hour, the Union lost 1,800 men, including General McCook, three times the number of Confederate losses. Many soldiers were trapped on the hillside, now known as Cheatham's Hill, until nightfall. Sherman hoped to attack again the next day but was convinced by General Thomas that "one or two more such assaults would use up this army."

In his status report to Halleck, he noted, "As fast as we gain one position the enemy has another all ready, but I think he will soon have to let go Kenesaw [sic], which is the key to the whole country." Schofield extended his lines to the right throughout the 24th and 25th, but Johnston held on stubbornly, while Hood entrenched along the line he had occupied after the engagement at Kolb's Farm.

Sherman met with his three commanders on the 25th. He was concerned that the campaign was becoming a stalemate. In the month since New Hope Church his army had advanced 15 miles. He also felt that Johnston had become accustomed to his flanking moves and a frontal attack would be a surprise. "There was no alternative," he reported, "but to attack 'fortified lines,' a thing carefully avoided up to that time."

Sherman wanted the attack to appear to be an all-out assault across the entire Confederate front, preventing Johnston from shifting forces back and forth as the occasion dictated. On the left, McPherson's line stretched for four miles with Kennesaw and its companion Little Kennesaw Mountain, solidly held by Loring's corps, as its axis. Thomas, with the bulk of the troops on a compacted 2-mile front in the center, was directed to attack Hardee's corps at a place which would come to be named Cheatham Hill, after its defender. On the Federal right, Schofield confronted Hood along the Powder Springs Road. His task was to feint to the southeast.

Early on the 27th, following a furious cannonade, Blair and Dodge assaulted Kennesaw Mountain while Logan attacked what was believed to be the weaker point at Pigeon Hill. "Officers and men fell thick and fast," Morgan Smith reported. Staggered by the steepness of the ascent, the thickness of the brush, and a furious barrage of musket and artillery fire, they could get no closer than 10 yards to the main line. The attack failed in less than an hour and the men retreated to a line of rifle pits they'd captured earlier. Logan lost seven of his regimental commanders and suffered 629 casualties in all.

About a mile to the right, on Thomas's front, Newton's and Davis's divisions of Palmer's Corps advanced in two columns with Wagner's and Kimball's brigades on the left and Harker's on the right. Again, after capturing the enemy's rifle pits, and taking over 100 prisoners, the attack faltered. "Apart from the strength of the enemy's lines," Newton wrote, "our want of success is in great degree to be attributed to the thickets and undergrowth, which effectually broke up the formation of our columns and deprived that formation of the momentum which was expected of it." Newton reported 654 casualties, and Thomas overall lost 1,580, with "some of our men being shot while on the parapets of the enemy's works."

The battle of Kennesaw Mountain. Despite a furious cannonade, the main attack on Kennesaw Mountain on the 27th was a dismal failure for Sherman, and not one that would be repeated. (LOC)

Sherman called the battle "the hardest fight of the campaign up to that date." Among the more than 3,000 Union casualties were two brigade commanders: Brigadier-General Charles Harker; and Sherman's old law partner, Colonel Dan McCook. Johnston offered a tribute of sorts to the Federal troops: "The characteristic fortitude of the Northwestern soldiers held them under a close and destructive fire long after reasonable hope of success was gone." But they were no match for his men. They lost because "they encountered *intrenched* infantry unsurpassed by that of Napoleon's Old Guard, or that which followed Wellington into France, out of Spain."

As it turned out, Schofield's feint created the success of the day. The evening before, Schofield had directed Cox to send Reilly's brigade south along the Sandtown Road to Olley's Creek. Reilly occupied a range of hills on the north side of the creek and spotted Jackson's dismounted cavalry on the other side. Cox dispatched Byrd's brigade to cross the creek northeast of Jackson where it entrenched on a hill. Hood and Johnston were aware of the threat on the left, but were more concerned about the activity to their front.

At 4.00am on the 27th, four hours before the main attack along the Kennesaw line, Reilly and Byrd, now joined by Cameron's brigade, continued their advance, while Hascall's division pushed down the Powder Springs Road. Jackson's dismounted cavalry were clearly overmatched by Cox's infantry. By 8.30, the Federals had pushed the Rebels back over a mile and established a 4-mile-wide front. By the time the firing had died away to the north, Cameron and Reilly were digging in on a ridge overlooking the intersection of the Sandtown Road with the road from Marietta. Hood's line was visible through the trees to the north. To the east was Nickajack Creek, the last natural barrier between Sherman and the railroad, 3 miles away. Sherman recognized that Cox's location was the key to prying Johnston off Kennesaw Mountain.

Illinois Monument at the Dead Angle. The fiercest fighting of the day occurred at a salient in the Confederate line known today as the "Dead Angle." (Author's collection)

While both armies recovered from the fighting along the Kennesaw line, Sherman began issuing new orders. Hascall's division marched on the 1st, followed by Morgan Smith's division of XV Corps early the next day. This gave Schofield over 13,000 men in a strong position, 4 miles south of Hood's line, and only 6 miles north of the Chattahoochee. Johnston would have to pull his troops off Kennesaw Mountain, or risk being surrounded. The Confederate commander, reluctantly, came to the same conclusion.

Johnston ordered a withdrawal to begin at dusk. The timing was such that McPherson was pulling his troops out of their entrenchments on the north side of Kennesaw Mountain at the same time that Loring was extricating his men from the south side. Sherman was aware that his opponent was moving, and again was hopeful it was a withdrawal across the Chattahoochee. Early the next morning, Logan sent a skirmish line up the hill. Sherman watched as Union troops began appearing on the top of Kennesaw Mountain. Logan entered Marietta at 9.00am on July 3.

Sherman desperately wanted to catch Johnston's army fleeing in disarray across the river, but it was not to be. Hooker tried to elbow his way through Howard's Corps in an effort to be in front, forcing a delay as Howard had to countermarch to join up with Palmer. "Old Slow Trot" Thomas was his usual cautious self, refusing to be hurried. "We will never have such a chance again," Sherman wrote Thomas, "press with vehemence at any cost of life and material."

Major-General Benjamin Franklin Cheatham. On June 27, at the ridge that now bears his name, Cheatham's Division shattered the Federal attack. (LOC)

The new Confederate line had been readily prepared by Johnston's chief engineer, Colonel Stephen Prestman. Located at Smyrna Camp Grounds, between Marietta and the Chattahoochee River, it extended for 6 miles, from Rottenwood Creek on the right towards Nickajack Creek on the left. It was not Kennesaw Mountain, but it was enough to frustrate Sherman. Johnston was not ready to give up his hold north of the river quite yet.

Johnston's artillery chief, Brigadier-General Francis Shoup, was busy overseeing the construction of the next series of fortifications along the north bank of the Chattahoochee River, while Johnston held on at Smyrna. The "Shoup" line consisted of some three dozen log-and-earth forts extending for over 6 miles, covering Turner's Ferry and the Western & Atlantic railroad bridge. These "Shoupades" were interconnected by trenches and log palisades, and protected by artillery redans with interlocking fields of fire.

The Federals celebrated Independence Day by tightening the ring around Johnston. Howard advanced from Marietta while McPherson pushed Dodge farther east. Stanley's division of Howard's Corps, on the Federal left, captured the Rebel skirmish line at Smyrna, taking a number of prisoners. Leggett encountered Major-General Gustavus Smith's Georgia Militia on the Turner Mill Road, and Smith notified Johnston that he was facing overwhelming force. Late in the day, Hood, holding the left of the Smyrna line, reported that he was about to be flanked. Johnston sent Cheatham to his assistance, but now realized that Federal troops were closer to Atlanta than he was.

"During the night Johnston drew back all his army and trains inside the *tête-du-pont* at the Chattahoochee," Sherman wrote, "which proved one of the strongest pieces of field-fortifications I ever saw." Thomas advanced south along the main road from Marietta, with Schofield and McPherson to his right. Stoneman's cavalry moved 10 miles downriver towards Sandtown while Sherman sent Garrard 18 miles in the opposite direction towards Roswell.

Sherman admitted being caught completely off guard by the Shoup line, expecting Johnston to quietly slip away across the river. This time, however, "we held the high ground," Sherman noted, "and could overlook his movements, instead of his looking down on us."

From his vantage point, Sherman almost made the blunder of the campaign. Mistaking Johnston's supply trains on the south side of the river for the Rebel army's camp, "I came near to riding into a detachment of the enemy's cavalry." Later that day, Colonel Frank Sherman, one of Howard's staff officers, did exactly that. "For some time, the enemy supposed they were in possession of the commander-in-chief of the opposing army."

Johnston had his back to the wall, literally and figuratively. Sherman had refused to come at him head on, except at Kennesaw Mountain, an occasion that would not occur again. He had promised to go on the offensive when the situation permitted, but time was running out, and President Davis was seriously contemplating a change in leadership in the Army of Tennessee. As soon as Sherman put a sizable contingent across the Chattahoochee River, Johnston would have to fall back, and was already planning to use Peachtree Creek as his next barrier.

Johnston's problem was that he simply did not have the manpower to cover all of the possible river crossings that Sherman could use to interpose himself between Johnston and Atlanta. Sherman outnumbered him nearly 2:1, was able to maneuver around his opponent almost at will, and maintained his supply line along the railroad. "Johnston's army has heard the sound of our locomotives," Sherman told Halleck on the 6th.

Atlanta. On July 6, the Federal army approached the Chattahoochee River, and Sherman noted, "From a hill just back of Vining's Station I could see the houses in Atlanta, nine miles distant." (Author's collection)

THE BATTLES AROUND ATLANTA, JULY 6 TO SEPTEMBER 2, 1864

In his message to Halleck, Sherman laid out his strategy for the next phase of the campaign. "Instead of attacking Atlanta direct," he stated, "or any of its forts, I propose to make a circuit, destroying all its railroads." In the meantime, he ensured his own supply line was secure, repairing the railroad to Vining's Station, 8 miles south of Marietta and only 2 miles north of the river.

For the first time in the campaign, Sherman intended to pass around the Confederate right flank, rather than the left. Garrard's cavalry was in Roswell, 10 miles upriver, and had found a suitable place for a crossing. Meanwhile McCook led a small cavalry detachment above Soap Creek, between Peachtree Creek and Roswell, under the watchful eye of Wheeler. The disposition of the infantry followed the usual pattern; Thomas held the center against the Shoup Line, with McPherson on the right near Turner's Ferry.

Schofield crossed the Chattahoochee at Soap Creek, on the 9th. Garrard crossed at Roswell the same day, and both established strong defensive positions less than 5 miles north of Atlanta's defenses. Garrard was relieved by Newton's division, which was in turn relieved by Dodge's Corps. "That night Johnston evacuated his trenches," Sherman noted. The Peachtree Creek line was now the last barrier separating Sherman's armies from the defenses of Atlanta, but Johnston would not be the officer to defend it.

President Davis had never understood why Johnston had not gone on the offensive the minute he took over the Army of Tennessee in December. "My information led me to believe that the condition of the army, in all that constitutes efficiency, was satisfactory." Davis felt that "the men were anxious for an opportunity to retrieve the loss of prestige" caused by the demoralizing defeat at Missionary Ridge. Davis and apparently everyone else in the Confederacy watched as "Retreat followed retreat, during seventy-four days of anxious hope and bitter disappointment."

Bragg reported to Davis on July 14, after visiting Johnston's headquarters, "I cannot learn that he has any more plan for the future than he has had in the past." Davis asked Johnston, pointedly, "Will you surrender Atlanta without a fight?" Johnston's reply was "regarded as evasive." Davis had been

Chattahoochee River Bridge. Despite Johnston's best efforts to prevent Union troops from crossing the Chattahoochee River, this 780-foot-long, 90-foot-high railroad bridge was built in four and a half days. (LOC)

Operations around Atlanta, July 9 to September 1, 1864

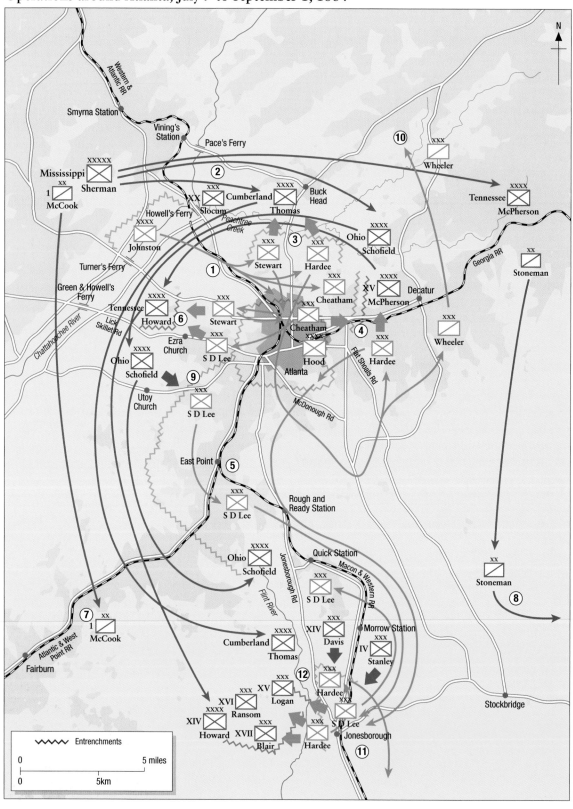

1. On July 9, upon learning that Sherman has two corps across the Chattahoochee River, Johnston orders his army to move to a new line south of Peachtree Creek.
2. Sherman begins his advance on Atlanta on July 17. Thomas crosses the Chattahoochee on pontoon bridges; while Schofield swings around Atlanta to the east; and McPherson moves further east toward Stone Mountain. Hood replaces Johnston as commander of the Army of Tennessee the next day.
3. Hood, hoping to catch the Federal army in the process of crossing Peachtree Creek, sends Stewart and Hardee to attack Thomas late in the afternoon of the 20th, while Cheatham covers Atlanta from the east. Stewart and Hardee are repulsed as Thomas digs in along the creek.
4. On July 22, believing that the Federal left flank is "in the air," Hood orders Hardee on a night march south through Atlanta. Stewart and Cheatham pull back into the inner defense line around Atlanta. Hardee attacks McPherson's Corps just after noon, while Wheeler rides for the Federal supply station at Decatur. Cheatham's Corps joins in the assault late in the afternoon, nearly succeeding in breaking the Federal line along the Georgia Railroad, but, again, the Confederates are repulsed. McPherson is killed in the attack and succeeded by Howard.
5. Having secured the Western & Atlantic Railroad to the north, and the Georgia Railroad to the east, Sherman determines to seize the railroad depot at East Point, cutting Hood's last supply line.
6. Hood learns of the move and, on July 28, and sends S. D. Lee and Stewart to Ezra Church in an effort to blunt the advance. Rather than remaining on the defensive, Lee orders an attack and is defeated, although he manages to maintain control of the vital Lick Skillet Road, blocking Howard's route to East Point.
7. Simultaneous with Howard's advance, Sherman orders a two-pronged cavalry attack at Lovejoy's Station, 20 miles south of Atlanta. McCook's division rides southwest to Fayetteville and turns east, while Stoneman's division rides southeast to McDonough.
8. While McCook attacks Lovejoy's Station on the 28th, as directed, Stoneman veers off towards Macon and Andersonville, in an attempt to free Union prisoners from two Confederate prisoner-of-war camps. He is surrounded and captured outside Macon with about one-third of his force.
9. At the beginning of August, Sherman directs his three subordinate armies to begin a sweep to the west and south of Atlanta to sever the remaining rail links into the city. On August 4, Schofield attacks S. D. Lee's Corps at Utoy Church, only to be repulsed.
10. On August 10, "Wheeler's Raid" begins, as 4,000 Confederate cavalry cross the Chattahoochee River at Roswell, and follow the Western & Atlantic Railroad north into Tennessee, tearing up the track and destroying Union supply depots. The raid has little effect on Sherman's move around the western side of Atlanta.
11. On August 31, six of Sherman's seven corps occupy an entrenched line within a mile of the Macon & Western Railroad at Jonesborough. Hardee and Lee attack but are pushed back. Hood, believing that the real Federal attack is going to come at Atlanta from the north, calls back Lee's corps, which marches toward East Point.
12. On September 1, Howard and Thomas attack Hardee, forcing him to withdraw to Lovejoy's Station. Hood, with his last supply line cut, evacuates Atlanta. Union troops occupy the city the next day.

wary of, to use Lincoln's campaign slogan for that year, "changing horses in midstream," but Johnston's answer and attitude "brought the President over." On July 17, Cooper notified Johnston that, "you have failed to arrest the advance of the enemy." More importantly, "you express no confidence that you can defeat or repel him. You are hereby relieved from the command of the Army and Department of Tennessee."

Davis now faced the task of finding a suitable replacement. Hardee had been offered and had refused the position in December, prompting the assignment of Johnston. Hardee would later state that by turning down the initial offer he had not wanted to exclude himself from being reconsidered. The logical appointee was Hood, who had been complaining about Johnston's unwillingness to commit his forces to battle to anyone who would listen, for some time. "It is natural to suppose that we have had several chances to strike the enemy a decisive blow. We have failed to take advantage of such opportunities." Hood assumed the command on the 18th, messaging Johnston, "Much to my surprise I received the appointment."

Sherman found out about the change from a Union spy on the 18th. He asked Schofield, Hood's West Point classmate, about the new commander and learned that "he was bold even to rashness." Encouraged that he might finally get a chance to fight the enemy on open ground, he cautioned his men to "be constantly ready for sallies." Sherman had admired Johnston and later commented, "The Confederate Government rendered us most valuable service."

Lieutenant-General John Bell Hood. Johnston expressed his opinion of the wisdom of selecting Hood as his replacement in a message to Samuel Cooper, "Confident language by a military commander is not usually regarded as evidence of competency." (LOC)

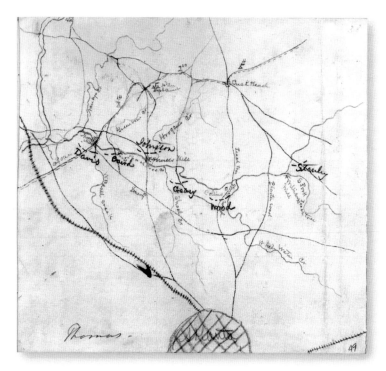

The battle of Peachtree Creek: "On the 17th we began the general movement against Atlanta, Thomas crossing the Chattahoochee at Power's and Paice's, by pontoon-bridges," Sherman reported. (LOC)

With his army converging on Atlanta on the 19th, and encountering virtually no resistance, Sherman entertained the possibility that Hood might actually be giving up the city. The Federal armies were moving "on a general right wheel." Thomas formed a line of battle along Peachtree Creek, 3 miles north of the city. McPherson had swung wide to the east, reaching the Georgia Railroad between Stone Mountain and Decatur, before turning towards Atlanta, 5 miles to the southwest. Schofield advanced on a road between his two co-commanders, but closer to McPherson, creating a gap between himself and Thomas.

Hood met with Johnston immediately after the change of command to discuss the overall situation. Johnston laid out his somewhat belated plan for attacking the Federal armies. "First," Johnston explained, "I expected to engage the enemy on terms of advantage while they were divided in crossing Peach-Tree Creek." Hood concurred.

He deployed his forces with Stewart, the recently appointed commander of Polk's Corps, on the left, Hardee in the center, and Cheatham, the new

Tanyard Branch at Collier's Mill. The center of fighting at the battle of Peachtree Creek occurred here on July 20, 1864. (Author's collection)

commander of Hood's Corps, on the right. Wheeler patrolled the extreme right. "My object was to crush Thomas's army before he could fortify himself, and then turn upon Schofield and McPherson." The attack was scheduled to go off at 1.00pm on the 20th, before Thomas could have all of his army south of the creek, but Hood discovered that Logan's XV Corps was advancing along the railroad faster than he had anticipated, and ordered his whole line to shift to the right, delaying the attack until 3.30pm.

Sherman was concerned about the gap between Thomas and Schofield, and sent Howard, with Stanley and Wood, to connect with Schofield's right, leaving Newton dangling on Thomas's left flank. Thomas was in the midst of crossing Peachtree Creek on the morning of the 20th, as Johnston had predicted, well separated from Schofield and McPherson, giving Hood the opportunity he was waiting for. The attack was to be "by division in echelon from the right, at a distance of about 150 yards," Hood directed, "the effort to be to drive the enemy back toward the creek, and then toward the river." Thomas would be trapped between Peachtree Creek and the Chattahoochee, but timing was everything. "They came surging on through the woods, down the gentle slope, with noise and fury," Howard reported, "like Stonewall Jackson's men at Chancellorsville." But the delay had allowed most of Thomas's army to get across the creek and begin digging in.

Bate's Division, on Hardee's right, began the attack, and by chance, ran into the gap between Thomas and Schofield. They got lost in the woods, were enfiladed by Union artillery north of the creek, and accomplished nothing. Walker, to Bate's left, charged towards a narrow ridge-line one half-mile south of the creek occupied by Newton's 2,700-man division. Kimball's and Blake's brigades had barely thrown up log and rail barricades, when they were hit. Bradley's brigade held Newton's left where Bate's division would have been if it had not become disoriented. Maney's division came in on Newton's right, completely overlapping his right flank, but Kimball turned 90 degrees to the right and forced Maney back and into the path of Ward's division of Hooker's Corps, which was just coming into line. Despite repeated attempts over the next several hours, none of Hardee's divisions was able to break through.

Loring's division, to Maney's left, was the first of Stewart's Corps to become engaged. They managed to carry the skirmish line in their front but were enfiladed on their right, again by Ward's division after Maney's attack failed. Scott's brigade of Loring's division had better success, overrunning the 33rd New Jersey, which occupied, as Geary described it, "a high, narrow, timbered hill in front of my right." Loring called for Cleburne's division, being held in reserve, to press his

Major-General George Henry Thomas. The troops called him "Old Slow Trot," for his deliberate pace, but Sherman relied on him to lead the center of the advance, and his men performed admirably throughout the campaign. (LOC)

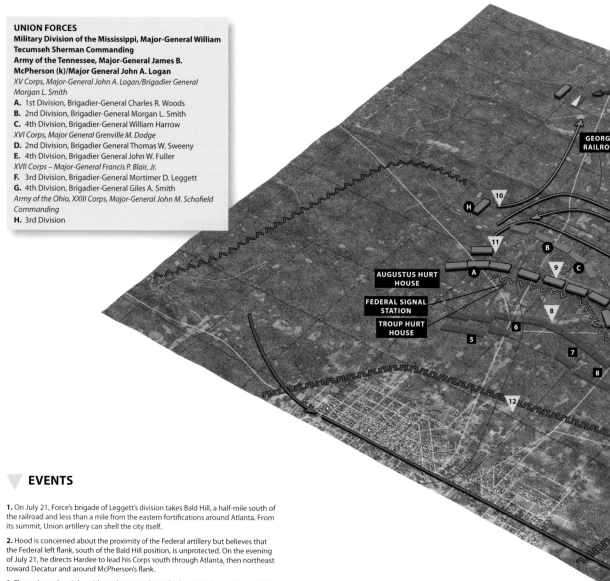

UNION FORCES
Military Division of the Mississippi, Major-General William Tecumseh Sherman Commanding
Army of the Tennessee, Major-General James B. McPherson (k)/Major General John A. Logan
XV Corps, Major-General John A. Logan/Brigadier General Morgan L. Smith
A. 1st Division, Brigadier-General Charles R. Woods
B. 2nd Division, Brigadier-General Morgan L. Smith
C. 4th Division, Brigadier-General William Harrow
XVI Corps, Major General Grenville M. Dodge
D. 2nd Division, Brigadier General Thomas W. Sweeny
E. 4th Division, Brigadier General John W. Fuller
XVII Corps – Major-General Francis P. Blair, Jr.
F. 3rd Division, Brigadier-General Mortimer D. Leggett
G. 4th Division, Brigadier-General Giles A. Smith
Army of the Ohio, XXIII Corps, Major-General John M. Schofield Commanding
H. 3rd Division

GEORG
RAILRO

AUGUSTUS HURT
HOUSE

FEDERAL SIGNAL
STATION

TROUP HURT
HOUSE

▼ EVENTS

1. On July 21, Force's brigade of Leggett's division takes Bald Hill, a half-mile south of the railroad and less than a mile from the eastern fortifications around Atlanta. From its summit, Union artillery can shell the city itself.

2. Hood is concerned about the proximity of the Federal artillery but believes that the Federal left flank, south of the Bald Hill position, is unprotected. On the evening of July 21, he directs Hardee to lead his Corps south through Atlanta, then northeast toward Decatur and around McPherson's flank.

3. Throughout the night, with a column nearly 2 miles long, Hardee marches out from the McDonough Road, then turns northeast and arrives at Cobb's Mill at dawn on the 22nd. Hardee halts to allow the column to close up and give the men a brief rest.

4. Reaching a point along the Fayetteville Road near the widow Parker's house, still 6 miles from Decatur, by mid-morning, well past the time Hood was planning for the attack to begin, Hardee halts again to consult with his staff. Convinced that they must be well past the Federal left flank by now, Hardee faces his divisions to the north and begins the attack, while Wheeler's cavalry continues to Decatur to attack the Union supply station there.

5. At 12.15pm on July 22, Bate's and Walker's divisions, with no knowledge of the terrain, are forced to angle around Terry's Mill Pond. They emerge from deep woods approximately 1 mile southeast of the Georgia Railroad, unexpectedly encountering three brigades (Morrill, Mersy, and Rice) of Grenville Dodge's XVI Corps, which had been, coincidentally, hurried south by McPherson to cover his left flank. Walker and McPherson are both killed during the battle.

6. To their left, Cleburne's and Maney's divisions overwhelm Giles A. Smith's Federal division. Cleburne's men sweep north behind Smith's shattered troops and into the gap between the Federal XVI and XVII Corps towards Bald Hill.

7. After desperate fighting on both sides, Cleburne's attack falters at the foot of Bald Hill around 3.00pm.

8. At 3.30pm, Hood, who has been observing the attack from the Atlanta fortifications, sends in Cheatham's Corps, which moves eastward along the line of the Georgia Railroad. The new attacks hit Logan's XV Corps, which occupies the main north–south segment of the Federal line, extending from approximately a half-mile north of the railroad south to Bald Hill.

9. As Carter Stevenson's division presses Leggett's division around Bald Hill, Manigault's brigade of Brown's division breaks through the Federal line at the railroad. While the northern and southern tips of the Federal line struggle to maintain position, the center begins to fall back to the southeast, with Bald Hill, soon to be renamed Leggett's Hill, as the hinge.

10. Sherman, observing the battle from the vicinity of the Augustus Hurt House, orders Schofield's artillery, in line near his position, to open fire, thus enfilading the attacking Rebels.

11. Late in the afternoon, the Federal XV Corps mounts a counterattack, driving Cheatham's Corps back, and regaining the ground lost earlier in the battle.

12. At dusk, the fighting dies out and the Confederate troops withdraw behind the Atlanta fortifications.

THE BATTLE OF ATLANTA, JULY 22, 1864
Hood attacks McPherson's vulnerable left flank

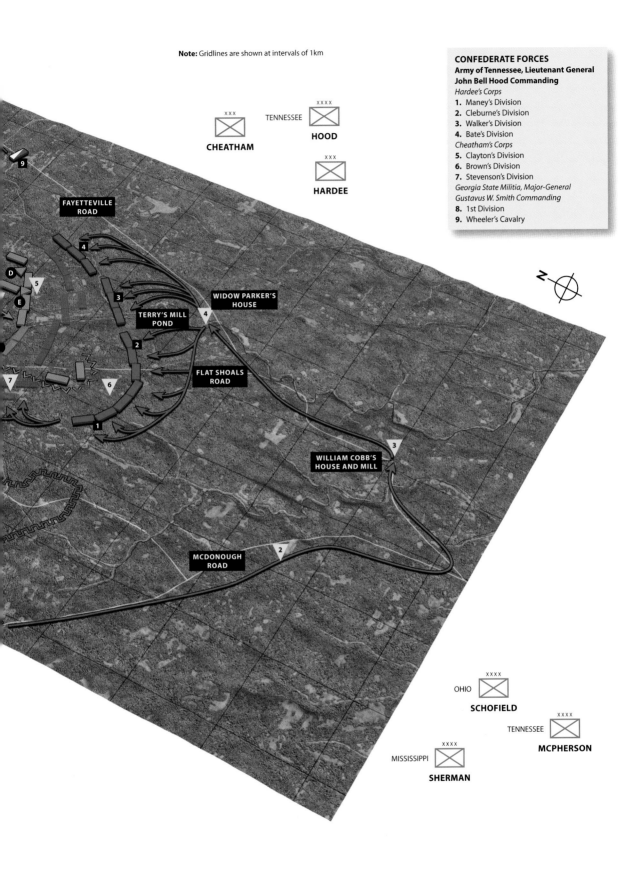

Note: Gridlines are shown at intervals of 1km

CONFEDERATE FORCES
Army of Tennessee, Lieutenant General John Bell Hood Commanding
Hardee's Corps
1. Maney's Division
2. Cleburne's Division
3. Walker's Division
4. Bate's Division
Cheatham's Corps
5. Clayton's Division
6. Brown's Division
7. Stevenson's Division
Georgia State Militia, Major-General Gustavus W. Smith Commanding
8. 1st Division
9. Wheeler's Cavalry

TENNESSEE

CHEATHAM

HOOD

HARDEE

FAYETTEVILLE ROAD

WIDOW PARKER'S HOUSE

TERRY'S MILL POND

FLAT SHOALS ROAD

WILLIAM COBB'S HOUSE AND MILL

MCDONOUGH ROAD

OHIO

SCHOFIELD

TENNESSEE

MCPHERSON

MISSISSIPPI

SHERMAN

advantage, but Hood had become concerned about McPherson's advance along the railroad from Decatur, and Cleburne was on his way to reinforce Cheatham east of Atlanta.

For the Federals, the crisis of the day raged around the hill now held by Scott's brigade. Candy's and Jones's brigades of Geary's division managed to drive Scott's Confederates back and reoccupy the high ground. O'Neal's Alabamans of Walthall's division charged their right flank and passed into their rear. In the chaos, several Union regiments abandoned the field, but Geary rallied his troops, and five regiments from Candy's, Ireland's and Jones's brigades organized around Geary's artillery. "These five regiments, with the aid of my batteries, fighting on all sides," held the hill throughout the battle. "For three hours the fury of the battle along our entire line could not be surpassed," Geary wrote. "Then the tempest of sounds and missiles began gradually to decrease, and by dark nothing but heavy skirmishing remained." Stewart's attack, like Hardee's, failed.

Hardee urged his commander to let him try again, but Hood recognized that his men had done all they could that day, and pulled back. Both sides had over 20,000 troops engaged, but Hood suffered the majority of the casualties, losing more than 2,500 men to Thomas's 1,750. Despite the new Confederate commander's desire to have everything go off smoothly, the attacks were disjointed. "I cannot but think," Stewart reported, "had the plan of the battle, as I understood it, been carried out fully, we would have achieved a great success."

Hood downplayed what was essentially a significant defeat in his report to Seddon that night. "At 3 o'clock to-day a portion of Hardee's and Stewart's corps drove the enemy into his breast-works, but did not gain possession of them. Our loss slight." Sherman's report to Halleck expressed the confidence of the victor. "For two hours the fighting was close and severe, resulting in the complete repulse of the enemy with heavy loss in dead and wounded." The Federal commander was more encouraged by the positions occupied by his artillery. "I will open on the town from the east and northeast to-morrow."

"The 21st, a fearfully hot day, was spent by all in readjustment," Howard noted. Thomas brought his three corps forward and the gap between the armies was filled. Schofield continued to advance north of the Georgia Railroad, and McPherson, "to get a better left, ordered Blair to seize Bald Hill," a key prominence barely a mile east of Atlanta's defenses. "I moved my division upon the enemy's works on the hill which I now occupy about sunrise," Brigadier-General Leggett reported. "Before 9 a.m. of that day I had a battery in position and

The rebel Line east of Atlanta. "From various parts of our lines the houses inside of Atlanta were plainly visible, though between us were the strong parapets, with ditch, *fraise, chevaux-de-frise,* and abatis, prepared long in advance." (LOC)

threw shells into Atlanta." His division suffered 365 casualties, including Brigadier-General Force, who led the attack and was severely wounded, joining Brigadier-General Gresham, who had been similarly wounded in Wheeler's defense of the hill the day before, the action that had caused Hood to pull Cleburne from his support of Stewart.

Hood did not mention the loss of Bald Hill to his superiors, but understood the significance of what McPherson had accomplished, and called in his lieutenants to give them their orders for the 22nd. "The position and demonstration of McPherson's army on the right threatening my communications made it necessary to abandon Atlanta or check his movements." He notified General Wright to be "prepared to-night for an evacuation of Atlanta, should it become necessary."

Wheeler reported that McPherson was overly focused on Atlanta in his front, leaving his left flank vulnerable. Hood pulled Stewart and Cheatham inside the city's fortifications, and dispatched Hardee on a night march to "completely turn the left of McPherson's army." Hardee was to march south out of the city at 1.00am, to be in place for an attack at daylight, and he was directed to go as far as Decatur if need be, to ensure he was well beyond McPherson's rear. Wheeler, covering his right, would continue to attack McPherson's supply train at Decatur. Cheatham, with Stewart following, would then join in the general assault to roll up the Federal line, and "continue to force the whole from right to left down Peach-Tree Creek."

Like the battle two days before, timing was everything. Cleburne had trouble extricating his division from his line without letting the Federals know that something was happening in their sector, and it was after 3.00am before the final elements of Hardee's corps exited the city. By the time the head of the column reached Cobb's Mill, 6 miles from Atlanta, and made its turn back to the north, it was already dawn. They stopped again to confer about noon, six hours behind schedule. Hardee was annoyed, and not above letting his subordinates know about it, chastising first Wheeler, then W. H. T. Walker when they tried to suggest alterations to the plan. "This movement has been delayed too long already," Hardee exclaimed, "Go and obey my orders!"

Hardee was convinced that he must be well beyond the Federal left flank. Brigadier-General George Maney, who had taken Cheatham's position following the latter's accession to corps command, and Cleburne, to his right, led their respective divisions north, directly toward Bald Hill. Farther right, and separated by deep woods, W. H. T. Walker and Bate encountered thick underbrush and rough terrain. Wheeler continued to Decatur.

Walker had argued with Hardee about finding another route around the briar patch his men were now struggling through, and he was getting angrier by the minute. Hearing the sound of guns to his left, he finally emerged from a stand of pines into what had been undefended terrain only 30 minutes earlier. Now, by pure chance, it was occupied by elements of Dodge's XVI Corps hurrying to the west. A Federal picket spotted a cluster of Rebels on his left and shot Walker from his horse, killing him instantly.

Dodge's men had spent the morning carrying out Sherman's order to tear up "every rail and tie of the railroad, from Decatur up to your skirmish line," and with their task complete, were moving to support Blair's XVII Corps, on their left. Alerted, by the picket firing, to the large body of Confederate troops moving north along Sugar Creek, Dodge halted the column, turned his men 90 degrees to face south, and formed a triple line. Bate's and Walker's divisions, the latter now under the command of Brigadier-General Hugh Mercer, emerged from the woods. The Federals fired and stopped the two Rebel divisions in their tracks.

Maney and Cleburne had somewhat better success. Maney, at first, came in too far to the west and overlapped the southern end of the Federal line, forcing him to turn hard right, directly into the face of the enemy's entrenchments. Cleburne managed to hit the Federals edgewise and drove them back. Major-General Giles Smith's division was caught in a pincer and forced to retreat to the Federal works on Bald Hill, where it joined its line to that of Brigadier-General Mortimer Leggett.

McPherson was conferring with Sherman at his headquarters north of the railroad when the attack began. Reports had been coming in all morning that "the enemy has evacuated his works around Atlanta," and Sherman, believing that the Rebels were giving up the city, was issuing orders to each of his lieutenants to "put your command in pursuit." The sound of guns off to the southeast took them by surprise.

McPherson rode off and quickly came in sight of the fighting near the point where Dodge had first encountered Bate's and Mercer's troops. He dispatched his staff officers to Blair and Dodge, with orders to stand fast, then started heading in the direction of Bald Hill. Suddenly, he found himself, with only his orderly, face to face with a group of Rebel skirmishers. An Arkansas captain demanded their surrender. McPherson made as if to comply, then spurred his mount and attempted to get away. He was shot through the

The death of McPherson. This much-stylized depiction of McPherson's death is more reflective of his popularity. Sherman noted he was "in his prime … universally liked, and had many noble qualities." (LOC)

back and died almost immediately. When asked by the Rebel captain who the dead officer was, the orderly replied tearfully, "Sir, it is General McPherson. You have killed the best man in our army."

Sherman was almost overwhelmed with sadness by the death of the man many believed to be the rising star in the Union Army, and expressed his grief in a letter to McPherson's fiancée. "I yield to no one but yourself the right to exceed me in lamentations for our dead hero." In the meantime, he had a battle to fight. He assigned temporary command of McPherson's army to Major-General John "Black Jack" Logan, directed Schofield to send one brigade to Decatur to assist Sprague, who was fighting off Wheeler; and dispatched two additional brigades to support Dodge's corps along the railroad. The main fight was left in the hands of Logan and the Army of the Tennessee, which Sherman believed would want to revenge its former commander's death. "Nobly did they do their work that day, and terrible was the slaughter done to our enemy, though at sad cost to ourselves."

Hood had been impatiently waiting for the battle to develop since dawn. From his observation post at the Oakdale Cemetery, on the eastern side of Atlanta, he could see Maney's attack appear to falter a mile away. If Maney was attacking the southwestern corner of the Union line, it could mean only that Hardee had not attacked McPherson's rear, as ordered, but his front. Around 3.30pm, Hood ordered Cheatham to go forward along the Georgia Railroad and assault the main north–south axis of the Union line, now held by the XV Corps. The Georgia Militia, under Major-General Gustavus Smith, joined in the attack on Cheatham's right flank, charging Bald Hill.

Major-General Gustavus Smith. Smith led the Georgia State Militia during the campaign. He commanded the Army of Northern Virginia for one day before being succeeded by Robert E. Lee. (LOC)

Manigault's brigade of Hindman's division hit the area of the line most recently held by Martin's brigade of the 2nd Division, which had been sent by Logan to the assistance of XVI Corps. According to Lieutenant-Colonel Townes, Chief of Staff of XV Corps, "the attack was in such force that the line gave way and the guns and horses of De Gress' Battery (H), 1st Illinois Light Artillery, four 20-pounder Parrotts, with two brass pieces (12-pounders) were captured by the enemy." Brigadier-General Charles R. Woods, commanding the 1st Brigade, immediately directed another battery to open fire on the artillery horses, managing at least to prevent the Parrotts from being hauled away. He then mounted a furious counterattack, retook the guns and turned them, once more, "on the discomfited enemy, which he did with most terrible effect, as they were moving off the field in confusion."

The repulse of Cheatham's attack was aided in large part by Sherman himself, from his headquarters just north of the line of battle. Woods went to Sherman in person to report that the line had been "swept back." Sherman ordered him to "wheel his brigades to the left, to advance in echelon, and to catch the enemy in flank." To aid the counterattack, Sherman directed Schofield to open with his batteries, 20 guns in all, over the heads of the attacking Federals. "These combined forces drove the enemy into Atlanta," Sherman reported.

The fighting around Bald Hill stood as testimony to the stubbornness of the Union defenders and Sherman's faith in the Army of the Tennessee. "The enemy broke through," Leggett reported of Cleburne's attack just after noon. "I immediately put my men upon the other side of their works, their foes to the east and their backs to Atlanta." A succession of attacks caused them to jump back over to the east side, and at times, face to the south. "The hill must be retained at all hazards and at whatever cost," Leggett told his men. By the time Cheatham's attack came, "our men were greatly fatigued with about five hours' hard fighting." In this last engagement of the day, the fighting became "a hand-to-hand conflict, the sword and the bayonet and even the fist, were freely and effectively used, and the enemy repulsed with a slaughter I never before witnessed."

Major-General Oliver Otis Howard. Sherman wrote that, "As soon as it was known that General Howard had been chosen to command the Army of the Tennessee, General Hooker applied to be relieved of his command of the Twentieth corps, and General Thomas forwarded his application to me approved and *heartily* recommended." (LOC)

XVII Corps suffered 760 casualties on the 22nd, and 1,125 over the two days of fighting, but the newly rechristened Leggett's Hill was retained, much to the discomfiture of Hood, who finally had to admit, at least to himself, defeat. He underplayed the battle in his message to Secretary Seddon, so well that it came across as a victory, reporting that Hardee attacked the enemy's extreme left and "drove him from his works, capturing 16 pieces of artillery and 5 stand of colors." With regard to the late afternoon's action, Cheatham "drove the enemy, capturing six pieces of artillery." He was circumspect on his report of casualties, stating simply, "loss not fully ascertained." Best estimates put that number at around 5,000, compared with 3,500 on the Union side. It was a staggering loss.

"I am now grouping my command to attack the Macon road," Sherman wired Halleck on July 25. As a result of the battle of Atlanta, he controlled the area north and east of the city, leaving the Atlanta & West Point Railroad as Hood's only lifeline. Five miles south of Atlanta, the railroad split at East Point, with the Atlanta & West Point branch continuing southwest to Montgomery, Alabama, while the Macon & Western Railroad passed through Jonesborough to Savannah. Howard, the newly appointed commander of the Army of the Tennessee, was tasked with the assignment.

The decision to appoint Howard to his new position proved highly controversial. Logan had performed extremely well after taking over from McPherson on the 22nd, and, as the senior officer available in the Army of the Tennessee, certainly felt deserving of the post. His fault, according to Cox, was "his querulousness and disposition to find fault with commands given to him." There was no denying his ability to lead men in battle or his own personal gallantry, however. Hooker, having been at one time the commander of the Army of the Potomac, was senior to both Sherman and Thomas, and "looked upon the appointment to the vacancy as his right." Hooker's attitude, and the incident with Schofield at Kolb's Farm, remained on Sherman's mind, and, after consulting with Thomas, he recommended Howard to the President, who made the appointment.

This proved too much for Hooker. Howard had served under him in the Army of the Potomac, and it was Howard's XI Corps which had collapsed under the weight of Stonewall Jackson's magnificent flank attack, leading to Hooker's defeat at Chancellorsville. Hooker's request to be relieved was granted, and he left to become commander of the Northern Department, in Cincinnati, Ohio, while Major-General Henry W. Slocum, another former Hooker subordinate, was given command of XX Corps.

New appointments were desperately needed in Hood's army. The death of W. H. T. Walker on July 22 left a vacancy in Hardee's Corps, but it was decided that his division had been so broken up by the recent fighting, that it was more expedient to reassign Walker's regiments to other divisions. When Cheatham declined the permanent command of Hood's old corps, Lieutenant-General S. D. Lee, the commander of Confederate forces in Mississippi and Alabama, traveled from Montgomery to assume the post. In the midst of the turmoil, Hardee asked to be reassigned on account of his dissatisfaction with the elevation of Hood, but was persuaded by Davis to stay on.

The Confederate President, and indeed, much of the South, was convinced that the battle on the 22nd had been a great victory. On the 25th, Bragg told Davis that the "moral effect of our brilliant affair of the 22d has been admirable on our troops." Robert E. Lee noted: "if the news of the glorious victory at Atlanta, reported this morning, prove true it will again open to us Alabama and Mississippi." Their "celebration" was short lived. On the afternoon of the 27th, reports began to come in that the enemy was on the move to the west.

Howard began to pull out of his lines east of Atlanta on the night of July 26, and the next day marched around Schofield and Thomas to Proctor's Creek. By 10.00am on the 28th, Dodge's XVI Corps formed the left of a two-and-a-half-mile front, 3 miles west of the city. Blair's XVII Corps held the center, with Logan's XV Corps on the right. Between Blair and Logan was "an old meeting-house called Ezra Church near some large open fields by the poor-house on a road known as the Bell's Ferry road or Lick Skillet road." Dodge and Blair faced east, north of the church, while Logan's Corps held an angle, arcing southeast to southwest, just north of the road. When Hood became aware of the Federal movement, he ordered Lee to hold the enemy in check, "to prevent him from gaining the Lick Skillet road."

Sherman rode his entire line that morning and noted that his troops were everywhere busy in "throwing up the accustomed pile of rails and logs which after a while assumed the form of a parapet." As an additional precaution, he had ordered Davis's division of Palmer's Corps to follow Howard and be prepared to come in on Howard's left flank should the need arise. Unfortunately, faulty maps caused Davis's men to get lost.

Sherman was readily expecting to see Davis's skirmishers appearing before noon, when he was surprised to find Confederate troops advancing in considerable force in front of Logan. He later admitted to being caught off guard once again because he did not believe that Hood would be able to extend his lines in time to meet the new Federal threat. Howard, familiar with Hood from their previous encounters on the battlefield, and from their West Point days, thought otherwise. He suggested a methodical advance with each division deploying, digging in, and extending its lines, before again moving forward. It was slow and plodding, but Sherman deferred. In the end, Howard's prescience saved the day.

Lee, the lead for what Hood hoped would be a surprise appearance on Sherman's flank, was himself surprised to run into Federal soldiers at the point he did. Worse yet, his adversary had had the foresight to construct a line of entrenchments. "On the 28th, about 11 a.m.," Lee reported, "I received orders to move out the Lick Skillet road and check the enemy, who was then moving to our left." Logan's Corps was in the process of pushing its line south when the attack began. "During my advance in line of battle to a more desirable position," Logan reported, "we were met by the rebel infantry." Realizing that Federal troops were in the process of taking control of the road he had been sent to defend, Lee attacked, albeit with no idea of what was in his front. "His advance was magnificent," Sherman noted, "but founded on an error that cost him sadly."

Brown's division of Lee's Corps was first in, and managed to drive the Federals back over 500 yards to their previously established breastworks. "The woods were so dense," Brown reported, "that these works were not discovered until my line was upon them." Logan reacted with his usual coolness, strengthening the line at the point of attack. "In many places the works were carried," Brown continued, "but the enemy re-enforced so rapidly and with such an immensely superior force that my troops were driven with great slaughter from them." His division suffered over 800 casualties before withdrawing to a crest north of the road.

Ten minutes behind Brown, Clayton's division came in on Brown's right, and, according to Lee, "met with similar results." Walthall's division of Stewart's Corps had followed Brown and Clayton down the Lick Skillet Road, and "at my suggestion," Lee wrote, "was thrown against the enemy where Brown had attacked." The effort, he concluded, "was a failure." Stewart himself was wounded, as was General Loring. By 3.30pm, Lee pulled back. The battle of Ezra Church was a crushing defeat for Hood. Lee's Corps suffered over 3,000 casualties compared with about 600 on the Federal side. Strategically, however, he managed to maintain control of the Lick Skillet Road, preventing Howard from reaching the railroad. As it turned out, that was only one of Sherman's problems that day.

Howard's advance was to have occurred simultaneously with a two-pronged cavalry attack on the Macon & Western Railroad 20 miles south of Atlanta. General Stoneman was given command of his own and General Garrard's cavalry, a force of about 5,000 men, and directed to ride southeast of Atlanta to McDonough. General McCook, with his own and General Rousseau's cavalry, about 4,000 men in total, was to ride southwest to the city of Fayetteville. "They were to meet on the Macon road near Lovejoy's and destroy it in the most effectual manner," Sherman wrote. The attack went wrong from the start.

Before the raid, Stoneman had asked Sherman for permission to proceed to Macon and Andersonville and free the Federal prisoners there. Sherman consented, on the contingency that Stoneman first join with McCook to attack the rail line. McCook arrived at Lovejoy's Station on the 28th, but called off the raid when Stoneman failed to appear. Stoneman, for reasons known only to himself, headed directly for Macon, where he became trapped and captured with about 500 of his men, becoming the highest-ranking Federal officer to be taken prisoner during the war. The remainder of his force managed to make its way back to Atlanta. Stoneman was exchanged three months later at the personal request of Sherman, and was back in action by December.

The raid was a complete failure for Sherman, and forced him to reconsider his strategy for concluding the campaign. "I now became satisfied that cavalry could not, or would not, make a sufficient lodgment on the railroad below Atlanta." He would have to use his infantry to sever Hood's supply route. "The month of July closed with our infantry line strongly intrenched, but drawn out from the Augusta road on the left to the Sandtown road on the right, a distance of full ten measured miles." He recorded a loss of 9,719 killed, wounded, and missing in a month which "had been one of constant conflict, without intermission."

Hood made little mention of the affair at Ezra Church, preferring to focus, quite understandably, on his cavalry's success against Stoneman and

Major-General George Stoneman. Stoneman's capture following his abortive raid on Macon, Georgia, helped convince Sherman that cavalry was not the answer to destroying the railroads around Atlanta. (LOC)

McCook. His ability to mount any future offensive operations was severely hampered by the three battles fought between July 20 and 28, however. His "effective total present" strength on July 31 was reported as 44,495, down from 54,085 on June 30, a net loss of nearly one-fifth of his fighting capability. By comparison, Sherman reported an effective strength of 91,675 on July 31, compared with 106,070 a month earlier. Staggering numbers, by any means, but his ratio of combat-ready troops to Hood's had actually increased. Hood could ill afford many more "victories" like those that closed out the month.

At the beginning of August, Sherman designated Schofield's XXIII Corps as the lead element for "a bold attack on the railroad, anywhere about East Point," with Palmer's XIV Corps in support. Moving from the Federal left flank to the right, Schofield was in position north of Utoy Creek, halfway between Atlanta and East Point on August 2. "On the 3d General Hascall crossed Utoy Creek at Herring's Mill against strong resistance, and found the enemy occupying a strongly intrenched position in our front."

In the midst of the deployment, General Palmer asked to be relieved, on account of his belief that he outranked Schofield. Sherman tried to convince him to stay on, but, in the end, consented to his resignation, replacing him with Brigadier-General Jefferson Davis. Schofield finally attacked the heavily fortified position on the 6th, and achieved nothing. After a second attempt the next day, he withdrew. The engagement at Utoy Creek ended with 850 Union casualties versus less than three dozen on the Confederate side. It was, according to Sherman, "a noisy, but not a bloody battle."

Sherman was clearly frustrated. In his August 7 dispatch to Halleck, he noted, "I am too impatient for a siege." He ordered the intensity of the shelling of Atlanta, which had begun on July 20, to pick up, and on August 10, two 30-pdr Parrotts, the most commonly used siege gun in the Union Army, were added to his arsenal. Sherman had decided that "whether we get inside of Atlanta or not, it will be a used-up community when we are done with it."

He had also come to the realization that Hood's army could build fortifications faster than his army could move to get around them. "I may have to leave a corps at the railroad-bridge, well intrenched," he told Halleck, "and cut loose with the balance to make a circle of desolation around Atlanta." The result, he hoped, would be to "decoy him out to fight us on something like equal terms."

Thirty-pounder Parrott. Capable of firing a 4.2-inch, 30-pound shell up to 4,400 yards, Sherman noted that "we can pick out almost any house in town." (LOC)

On August 12, Sherman learned of two events. "I heard of the success of Admiral Farragut in entering Mobile Bay, which was regarded as a most valuable auxiliary to our operations at Atlanta." Farragut's victory caused elation in the North, and no more so than among Lincoln's supporters, who finally had something to point to with the election less than three months away. The second bit of news concerned Davis's endorsement of Hood's plan to disrupt Sherman's supply lines. "If he can be forced to retreat for want of supplies," Davis wrote, "he will be in the worst condition to escape or resist your pursuing army."

"Wheeler's Raid" had begun two days before. Crossing the Chattahoochee at Roswell with about 4,000 men, Hood's cavalry commander "tore up the railroad a few miles above Marietta," before proceeding through Cassville to Calhoun. There, Colonel Hannon's brigade captured over 1,000 head of cattle and returned with them to Atlanta. Wheeler continued north, with moderate success, beyond Chattanooga almost to Knoxville, before finally turning back. For a month, he "averaged 25 miles a day [and] swam or forded 27 rivers," but the Federal work crews repaired the tracks almost as fast as Wheeler's men could tear them up. In the end, the raid was more damaging to Hood, depriving him of half his cavalry during the critical closing stages of the campaign, than to Sherman, who reported having the minor annoyance of losing his communications with Nashville for a few days. Hood was forced to conclude, "no sufficiently effective number of cavalry could be assembled in the Confederacy to interrupt the enemy's line of supplies to an extent to compel him to retreat."

On August 13, Sherman directed XX Corps to draw back to the Chattahoochee River Bridge, "to protect our trains, hospitals, spare artillery, and the railroad depot." His other six corps, numbering some 70,000 men, prepared to "move to some point on the Macon railroad below East Point." Hood, in the dark about Sherman's intentions, reported to Seddon, "there is no material change to report in the enemy's position. He still evinces a desire to extend his right." On the 19th, Brigadier-General Ross reported that he was, "convinced the enemy I have been fighting is Kilpatrick's division on a raid."

With Wheeler's departure, Sherman decided to press what he believed was an advantage of cavalry in his favor. He suspended "the general movement of the main army," and sent Kilpatrick to break up the Macon Road "around Jonesboro." The affair was nearly a disaster, as Kilpatrick's division was surrounded and had to mount what some reports called "the greatest cavalry charge of the war" to fight their way out. Like Hood, Sherman "became more than ever convinced that cavalry" was not the answer. He resolved, "at once to proceed to the execution of my original plan."

On the 23rd, Sherman notified Thomas, Schofield, and Howard of his intent to march, "just after dark," on the 25th. Not above a little military deception, he wired Halleck to "give currency to the idea that I am to remain quiet till events transpire in other quarters, and let the idea be printed, so as to reach Richmond in three days. You understand the effect." On the 24th, satisfied that XX Corps could hold the Chattahoochee River Bridge, he telegraphed Halleck of his intent to "commence the movement around Atlanta by the south, to-morrow night, and for some time you will hear little of us." On the 28th, he reported, "Army of the Tennessee is on the West Point railroad near Fairburn; Army of the Cumberland is on the same road at Red Oak; and that of the Ohio will be to-night at Camp Creek." More importantly, "Enemy has made no serious opposition to our movement."

Hood was desperate for information. He notified Seddon on the 26th that Sherman had abandoned his lines east of Atlanta, but had not extended his right, and the next day reiterated that the enemy had "no troops nearer than four miles of Atlanta." He cautioned his corps commanders to remain vigilant, but was

Brigadier-General Hugh Judson Kilpatrick. His cavalry had demonstrated "so much zeal and activity," in a raid on the Atlanta & West Point Railroad, that Sherman hoped he would do the same at Lovejoy's Station. (LOC)

MINTY'S CHARGE AT LOVEJOY'S STATION, AUGUST 20, 1864 (PP. 82–83)

For nearly a month, Sherman had been trying to extend his lines west and south around Atlanta in an attempt to cut off Hood's last remaining supply line. Hood matched him mile for mile, and Sherman realized that Hood could build fortifications faster than he could move to get around them. He finally formulated a plan to send six of his seven infantry corps towards Jonesborough, but before committing to it, decided to try one last cavalry raid. On August 18, he sent out Brigadier-General Judson Kilpatrick with the Third Brigade, Third Cavalry Division, and Colonel Robert Minty's and Eli Long's brigades of the Second Cavalry Division. First against the Atlanta & West Point Railroad, then against the Macon & Western Railroad, Kilpatrick's troopers destroyed small sections of track and burned a large cache of Confederate supplies. On August 20, in the midst of an attack at Lovejoy's Station, 20 miles south of Atlanta, they suddenly found themselves trapped between Confederate Brigadier-General Alexander Reynolds's infantry brigade in their front and Brigadier-General Sul Ross' cavalry brigade, 800 yards in their rear. Determined to attempt a breakout before they could be completely surrounded, Kilpatrick tasked Colonel Minty with leading the charge.

With no clear idea of the size of the force against them, Minty turned his command about, toward Ross's dismounted Texans, and formed his 4,700 troopers in three columns by regiment, four riders abreast per column. The scene shows the 4th US Cavalry, which anchors the left **(1)** with the 4th Michigan **(2)** in the center and 7th Pennsylvania **(3)** on the right. Behind them is Long's brigade, from left to right, the 1st, 3rd, and 4th Ohio. Forming the third rank are the 3rd and 5th Kentucky, the 92nd Illinois Mounted infantry, and the Chicago Board of Trade artillery. Minty ordered sabers drawn and the advance began across an uncultivated field filled with gullies and ditches. The 700 men of Ross's Texas brigade **(4)** stand behind a rail fence, north of the McDonough Road, which is Minty's escape route. The rebels are supported by a single 12-pdr howitzer **(5)** on a hill amidst a stand of walnut trees across the road. The 4th US Cavalry angled to the left and hit the McDonough Road at full gallop, as the rest of the brigades followed behind. They crashed through the Texas brigade, as the lone Confederate cannon fired case shot and canister into their surging ranks. "Our men were mounted on the gallop and … cut them down right and left," recalled Captain Robert Burns of the 4th Michigan. Once they had broken through, the regiments turned and fired their Spencer carbine rifles into the woods and were hit with another round from the Confederates before they ran off. The charge was a success but the raid was a disaster, and Sherman gave orders for his infantry to begin their own advance less than a week later.

starting to hope that Sherman had actually begun a retreat north because of Wheeler's operations in his rear. When General Ross reported, "large wagon trains, tents, &c.," 5 miles below East Point, he was told, "General Hood does not think that there can be a large force advancing upon Jonesborough." Finally, on the evening of the 30th, Hardee convinced him that an attack was imminent. Hood was completely unaware of the size of the force facing Hardee when he wired him at 3.20am on the 31st, "You must not fail to attack the enemy as soon as you can get your troops up," and sent Lee to join him.

Twelve hours later, Hardee and Lee were in position, one half-mile west of Jonesborough. The battle plan called for an attack *en echelon* from the left. Hardee's own corps, under the tactical command of General Cleburne, was tasked with advancing towards the river, wheeling to the right and attacking the flank of the Federal XVI Corps. Once the attack was under way, Lee's Corps would advance straight ahead and assault Logan's XV Corps. Having heard the sounds of trains pulling into Jonesborough all night, Howard's men, straddling the Flint River, had ample time to dig in for the assault.

At the outset, Granbury's Texas Brigade, followed by Lowrey's and Mercer's brigades, encountered Kilpatrick's cavalry on the Federal right, veered to the left and drove them across the river, creating a gap in the Confederate line. Bate's division, losing its support on the left, was repulsed by Corse's entrenched Federals. Lee, taking Granbury's attack on Kilpatrick to mean that Cleburne's attack was well under way, ordered his corps forward. Stevenson's division, on the left, and Hindman's division, under the newly assigned Patton Anderson, on the right, overran the Federal skirmishers, but were repulsed by Logan's main line. Lee threw in his reserves, consisting of Clayton's division, with the same result. Hardee ordered Cleburne "to make no further attempt upon the enemy's works," and placed his forces on the defensive. Estimated losses on the Confederate side numbered around 1,700 compared with only 179 Federals.

That evening, Hood, unaware of Hardee's status because of the telegraph lines being cut, directed him to return Lee's corps to Atlanta. During the battle, Captain Buell, a member of Howard's staff, had been captured, and reported that Hardee was facing six of Sherman's corps. Hardee reported that Hood, "with a marvelous want of information, evidently still believed" that Sherman was preparing to attack Atlanta, and needed Lee's Corps for his protection. Overnight, Lee was pulled from the line and began his northbound trek.

On the morning of September 1, Hood was at Atlanta with Stewart's Corps and the Georgia Militia, Hardee was 30 miles south at Jonesborough, and Lee's corps was on the road from Jonesborough to Atlanta, "fifteen miles from each place, and in supporting distance of neither." Hardee set his lines with his back to the railroad, to meet Howard's advance. Sherman was with Howard when "General Davis formed his divisions in line about 4 P.M., swept forward over some old cotton-fields in full view, and swept over the rebel parapet handsomely, capturing the whole of Govan's brigade, with two field-batteries of ten guns." Stanley came up on Davis's left, but before they could advance, "darkness covered the field," Cox reported, "and put an end to the day's operations." Hardee suffered another 1,400 casualties, with losses on the Federal side numbering 1,272.

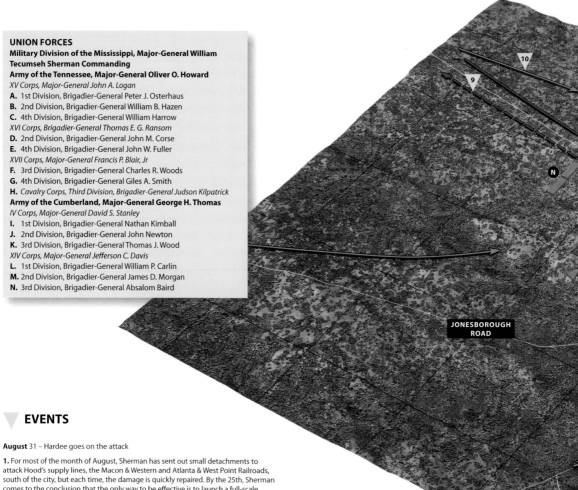

UNION FORCES
Military Division of the Mississippi, Major-General William Tecumseh Sherman Commanding
Army of the Tennessee, Major-General Oliver O. Howard
XV Corps, Major-General John A. Logan
A. 1st Division, Brigadier-General Peter J. Osterhaus
B. 2nd Division, Brigadier-General William B. Hazen
C. 4th Division, Brigadier-General William Harrow
XVI Corps, Brigadier-General Thomas E. G. Ransom
D. 2nd Division, Brigadier-General John M. Corse
E. 4th Division, Brigadier-General John W. Fuller
XVII Corps, Major-General Francis P. Blair, Jr
F. 3rd Division, Brigadier-General Charles R. Woods
G. 4th Division, Brigadier-General Giles A. Smith
H. *Cavalry Corps, Third Division, Brigadier-General Judson Kilpatrick*
Army of the Cumberland, Major-General George H. Thomas
IV Corps, Major-General David S. Stanley
I. 1st Division, Brigadier-General Nathan Kimball
J. 2nd Division, Brigadier-General John Newton
K. 3rd Division, Brigadier-General Thomas J. Wood
XIV Corps, Major-General Jefferson C. Davis
L. 1st Division, Brigadier-General William P. Carlin
M. 2nd Division, Brigadier-General James D. Morgan
N. 3rd Division, Brigadier-General Absalom Baird

JONESBOROUGH ROAD

▼ EVENTS

August 31 – Hardee goes on the attack

1. For most of the month of August, Sherman has sent out small detachments to attack Hood's supply lines, the Macon & Western and Atlanta & West Point Railroads, south of the city, but each time, the damage is quickly repaired. By the 25th, Sherman comes to the conclusion that the only way to be effective is to launch a full-scale assault on those routes. Consequently, he begins to transfer six of his seven corps from the north and east of Atlanta to the south and west. On August 30, after tearing up the Atlanta & West Point Railroad in the vicinity of Fairburn, Howard and Thomas turn east toward the Macon & Western Railroad at Jonesborough. Arriving at the Flint River, 1 mile west of the rail line, late in the afternoon, Logan's Corps drives Confederate skirmishers from the east side of the river, secures a lodgment on the high ground, and entrenches.

2. Kilpatrick crosses the river south of the main Federal position and advances on the town until halted by a small force of Confederate infantry just at nightfall.

3. Hood is aware that some troop movements are occurring, but is convinced that Sherman is actually withdrawing northward as a result of General Joseph Wheeler's cavalry attacks on Sherman's supply lines in that direction. Early on the 31st, as Sherman's forces move into position, Hood sends Hardee and Lee toward Jonesborough, while Stewart remains in Atlanta. Hood is convinced that Sherman has split his army and is vulnerable to attack. His plan calls for Hardee and Lee to destroy the smaller Union force to the south.

4. By the afternoon of the 31st, Logan, Ransom, and Blair have extended the Federal lines and are well entrenched, expecting an attack.

5. At 3.00pm, Hardee begins his attack *en echelon* from left to right. Lee's Corps, on the right, is to wait until Hardee's Corps is well-engaged with the main Federal line before attacking.

6. Cleburne's division encounters Kilpatrick's cavalry and veers to the left to drive them back across the river. In so doing, a gap is created in the line between Cleburne's division and Cheatham's (operating under the command of Maney), on the right.

7. Corse's entrenched division successfully repulses the attack of Maney and Bate's division (under the command of Brown).

8. Lee, mistaking Cleburne's attack on Kilpatrick for the signal to begin his own, goes in earlier than planned and is repulsed by Logan's Corps, with Ransom's in support. By nightfall, Hardee calls off any further attempts to breach the Federal line and falls back to his entrenchments west of the railroad.

September 1 – Thomas and Howard counterattack

9. Overnight, Lee's Corps is called back to East Point because of Hood's fear that Sherman still plans his main attack on Atlanta.

10. Throughout the night and into the morning of the 1st, Thomas arrives in several columns and takes position north of Jonesborough, along the railroad.

11. With Lee's Corps departed, Hardee adjusts his lines to face the new threat.

12. Late in the afternoon of the 1st, with Logan demonstrating on the right, and Blair advancing on the far right, Davis and Stanley attack, overwhelming the Confederate defenders. Govan's brigade is captured nearly intact, along with several artillery batteries, but the attack has gone off so late in the day that the Federal forces are unable to exploit their advantage before nightfall. Hardee withdraws south to Lovejoy's Station overnight, while Hood prepares to evacuate Atlanta.

THE BATTLE OF JONESBOROUGH, AUGUST 31 TO SEPTEMBER 1, 1864
Sherman attacks Hood's last supply line into Atlanta

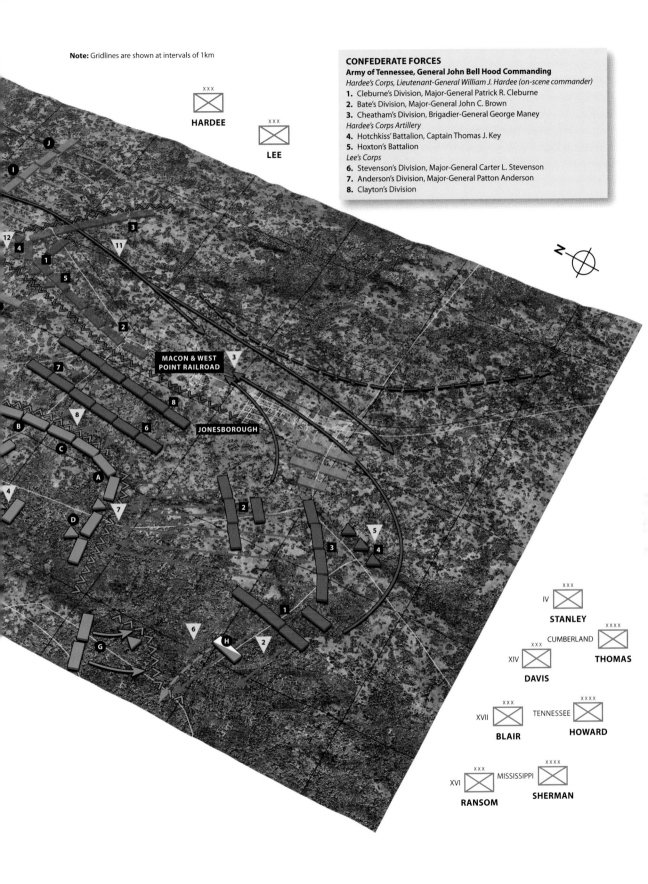

Note: Gridlines are shown at intervals of 1km

HARDEE

LEE

MACON & WEST
POINT RAILROAD

JONESBOROUGH

IV — STANLEY

CUMBERLAND — THOMAS

XIV — DAVIS

XVII — BLAIR

TENNESSEE — HOWARD

XVI — RANSOM

MISSISSIPPI — SHERMAN

Hood's Ordnance Train. Around midnight on September 1, Confederate cavalry, the last troops out of Atlanta, blew up 81 freight cars of ammunition, seven locomotives, and a rolling mill. (LOC)

"That night," Sherman noted, "I was so restless and impatient that I could not sleep." Through the night, Hardee retired his corps down the railroad to Lovejoy's Station. Having better communications with Davis in Richmond than with Hood in Atlanta, he recommended that Hood begin a general evacuation. Davis was not ready to surrender Atlanta yet, but Hood knew the time had come. Stewart's infantry led the march south at 5.00pm on September 1. Brigadier-General Ferguson's cavalry was the last to leave, destroying 81 freight cars of ammunition that Hood was unable to move. Sherman, near Jonesborough, heard the explosions.

Slocum ordered patrols to be sent out at dawn on the 2nd. One of these, under Colonel John Coburn, met a group of civilians led by Mayor James Calhoun, who announced that the Confederates were gone and requested a quick assumption of authority on the part of the Union Army to ensure law and order within the city limits. Coburn notified Slocum, who marched into the city around noon. Throughout the day, Sherman grew more anxious awaiting some confirmation of the situation. Finally, on September 3 at 6.00am, he was able to cable Halleck, "So Atlanta is ours, and fairly won."

AFTERMATH

When Sherman found out that Hardee had abandoned his lines at Jonesborough on the morning of September 2, he immediately set off in pursuit. IV Corps encountered "well-chosen and hastily constructed lines near Lovejoy's," but upon learning that Slocum occupied Atlanta, Sherman decided that his army was in need of a well-deserved rest, and pulled back. With Atlanta in his hands, he began to bring forward his stores from Allatoona and Marietta.

Hood reached McDonough, 50 miles southeast of Atlanta, by the middle of the afternoon on the 2nd, and dispatched Stewart to join Hardee at Lovejoy's Station, followed closely by Lee. Mary Boykin Chestnut noted in her diary the same day, "Atlanta indeed is gone. Well, that agony is over."

President Lincoln was magnanimous in his praise, noting that Sherman and his army were worthy of the "applause and thanks of the nation." Two months later, Lincoln would be re-elected in a landslide, winning not only the electoral vote, but the popular vote which had eluded him four years earlier, as well. His Democratic opponent resigned from the Army the same day.

Federal Fort. After the fall of Atlanta, Sherman instructed his Chief Engineer, Colonel Poe, to design an inner line of defense around the city, capable of being defended by a smaller garrison. (LOC)

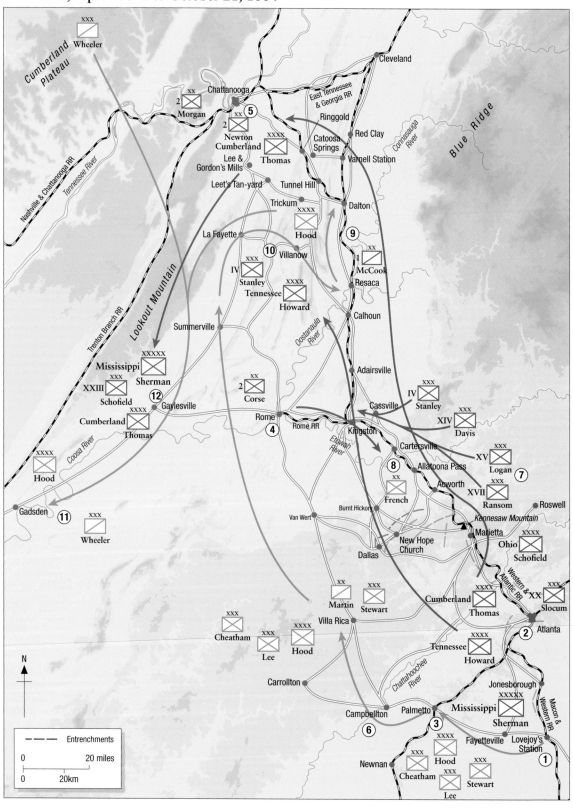

1. After evacuating Atlanta on September 1, Hood's Army of Tennessee, numbering 35,000, retreats toward Lovejoy's Station, 7 miles south of Jonesborough.
2. Slocum's XX Corps enters the city on the morning of the 2nd, and telegraphs Sherman of Atlanta's surrender.
3. For the next three weeks, the Federals rest and resupply. On the 21st, Hood moves 20 miles west to Palmetto where he meets with Confederate President Jefferson Davis on the 25th.
4. With Wheeler's Cavalry operating behind the Federal lines in Tennessee, Sherman dispatches Corse's division (XVI Corps) to Rome.
5. On the 29th, Thomas, with Morgan's division (XIV Corps), moves to Chattanooga, joining Newton's division (IV Corps), previously dispatched.
6. On October 1, Hood crosses the Chattahoochee at Campbellton.
7. Sherman, with Stanley and the remainder of IV Corps, Davis (XIV), Logan (XV), and Ransom (XVII), totaling 60,000 infantry and artillery, crosses the Chattahoochee on October 3 and 4 in pursuit.
8. On October 5, with Sherman advancing from Kennesaw Mountain, Hood sends French's Division of Stewart's Corps to seize the huge Federal supply depot at Allatoona, but is defeated by Corse's division, which arrives that morning by train from Rome.
9. Hood swings west, avoiding the Federal garrison at Rome, and, on October 12, attacks the garrison at Resaca, which has been reinforced by McCook's cavalry. Unsuccessful, Hood moves on, capturing Dalton on the 13th.
10. Sherman, hoping to bring Hood to bay, sends Howard through Snake Creek Gap to Lafayette on the 15th while Stanley advances from Villanow,
11. Hood, now reunited with Wheeler, avoids the trap, moving west and south through Gaylesville, and on the 17th, continues to Gadsden where he pauses for a week.
12. Sherman arrives in Gaylesville on the 21st. Here, he turns over the pursuit of Hood to Thomas and Schofield, while he prepares to return to Atlanta to direct the "March to the Sea."

Sherman's conquest, coupled with Farragut's "Damn the torpedoes! Full speed ahead!" victory (the latter phrase being shortened from the actual, but slightly less dramatic, "Four bells. Captain Drayton, go ahead, Jouett, full speed!") at Mobile Bay in August, was necessary and timely. Grant had Lee bottled up in what would be a tiresome siege at Petersburg, and even though Sheridan had won a messy campaign in the Shenandoah Valley, taking command from Franz Sigel and snatching victory from the jaws of defeat, Banks had been summarily beaten at Sabine Crossroads, and Butler was defeated by Beauregard at Drewry's Bluff. Lincoln needed Atlanta.

One of Sherman's first actions was to prepare to remove all civilians from the city and turn it into one vast military depot. "Atlanta is no place for families or non-combatants." Having seen firsthand the problems associated with trying to garrison "Memphis, Vicksburg, Natchez, and New Orleans," he wanted none of it.

Several days later, General Hood sent a request for a prisoner exchange, "out of the vast number of our men held captive at Andersonville." There were about 2,000 Confederate prisoners on their way to Chattanooga, and Sherman ordered them back to Atlanta. He offered to exchange them for "Stoneman, Buell, and such of my own army as would make up the equivalent, but I would not exchange for his prisoners *generally*." In other words, he would exchange only for Union soldiers of his department who had been captured during the campaign. His reasoning was that the 2,000 Confederate prisoners would be immediately reintegrated into Hood's army, but any Union prisoners not from Sherman's department would be sent north, back to their own units.

Hood was furious, and fired by his anger at Sherman's proposal to empty Atlanta of its citizens, started a bitter correspondence between the two commanders, some of which he had published in the newspapers. That very nearly ended any further discussion on either subject. Fortunately, reason prevailed and a neutral camp was established at Rough and Ready Station, where Lieutenant-Colonel Willard of Sherman's staff worked with Colonel Clare of Hood's staff to facilitate a number of prisoner exchanges, the "exodus" of the people of Atlanta, and generally to keep open the lines of communication between the two armies. Warner and Clare, at least, became good friends through their association.

On September 21, as Sherman was beginning to discuss his next operation with Grant, Hood moved his army 20 miles west, to Palmetto, Georgia. Three days later, Forrest attacked Athens, Alabama, capturing its garrison. With Hood's move west, Sherman was encouraged that central Georgia was "open for us to enter," a point that would play in his discussions with Grant, but he quickly realized that Hood's true purpose was to disrupt his supply lines to Tennessee. He quickly dispatched Newton's division of IV Corps to Chattanooga and Corse's of XVII to Rome.

One week later, after receiving a message from Grant telling him, "It will be better to drive Forrest out of Middle Tennessee as a first step," Sherman sent Thomas to Chattanooga. The last thing Sherman wanted was to chase Hood back through northwest Georgia, but on October 1, Hood's army crossed the Chattahoochee moving north, forcing his hand. Two days later, the Federal commander led elements of IV, XIV, XV, and XVII Corps, over 60,000 men, away from Atlanta.

Hood was causing as much trouble as he could, and Sherman, finding that the telegraph wires had been cut at Marietta, signaled, "over the heads of the enemy, a message for General Corse, at Rome, to hurry back to the assistance of the garrison at Allatoona," where over a million rations of bread were stored. Corse lost an ear and a cheekbone in defending the Allatoona garrison, but forced Hood to retire and go elsewhere.

On October 10, with Hood approaching the Etowah River, Sherman telegraphed Grant that he would, "infinitely prefer to make a wreck of the road and of the country from Chattanooga to Atlanta … and with my effective army move through Georgia, smashing things to the sea." Grant was not readily convinced and the chase continued as Hood attacked the garrisons at Resaca and Dalton, tearing up the railroad as he went. From Tunnel Hill, Hood turned south, hoping to draw Sherman into a battle, but was persuaded by his corps commanders that such a move was not in their best interests.

Sherman arrived at Gaylesville on the 21st, as Hood was passing through Gadsden, Alabama on his way to Decatur. By then, the Federal commander had had enough. He notified General Beckwith, the acting Quartermaster in Atlanta that "I want to prepare for my big raid. On the 1st of November I want nothing in Atlanta but what is necessary for war." He turned over the task of tracking down Hood to Thomas and Schofield, and made his way back to the city, where, on November 2, Grant finally approved his plan. "At 7 A.M. of November 16th," Sherman stated, "we rode out of Atlanta."

THE BATTLEFIELD TODAY

The Atlanta Campaign tour begins at Chattanooga, Tennessee, and ends at Jonesboro, Georgia. A list of roadside markers detailing the campaign is available at www.civilwarmarkers.com or www.georgiaplanning.com/hm. The Civil War Trust, at www.civilwar.org, has an Atlanta Campaign Battle App, with three tours extensively covering the available battle sites.

In the Chattanooga area, Chattanooga National Cemetery, Missionary Ridge, Lookout Mountain National Battlefield, and Chickamauga National Battlefield Park, although part of earlier campaigns, are worth the stop, and provide background for the Atlanta campaign.

Interstate 75 is the quickest, most direct, and busiest route, from Chattanooga to Atlanta. All of the battle sites are within a few miles of the highway, but US 41 is a much more enjoyable drive. There are markers, monuments, and points of interest at Ringgold (Ringgold Depot), Tunnel Hill (Clisby Austin House and Tunnel Hill), Mill Creek Gap (Fort Fisk), Resaca (Resaca Battlefield, Resaca Confederate Cemetery), Cassville (Cassville Cemetery), Etowah (Cooper's Furnace), Pine Mountain, Gilgal Church, Kolb's Farm, the Chattahoochee River (The "Shoupades"), and Jonesboro.

Kennesaw Mountain National Battlefield Park is the only national park site associated with the campaign on the tour. The battlefield is divided into segments, because of its location in the busy Marietta area, but those individual sites are worth the effort. The visitor center has information, maps, and a bookstore, as well as a short orientation film, all maintained by a well-trained staff.

Georgia maintains the Pickett's Mill Battlefield State Historic Site, which provides three fascinating walking tours, as well as an outstanding short film of the campaign. There is also a small museum and gift shop, all supported by an exceptional staff. Within a few miles are New Hope Church and Dallas.

The State of Georgia is developing a site of over 500 acres covering a portion of the Resaca Battlefield. See the Friends of Resaca Battlefield website, www.friendsofresaca.org, for information about the battlefield and the annual battle of Resaca reenactment.

There are a number of individual sites in and around the Atlanta area, but all are surrounded by city sprawl. The most fascinating is the Atlanta Cyclorama and Civil War Museum. The cyclorama was painted in 1885, and provides a 358-foot-wide, 42-foot-high view of the battle of Atlanta. It is in the process of being moved to the Atlanta History Center, which houses an excellent Civil War museum, in nearby Buckhead.

Information on the battle of Peachtree Creek is available in Tanyard Creek Park off Collier Road.

Mozley Park, off Martin Luther King Drive in west Atlanta, contains artifacts from the battle of Ezra Church.

Cascade Springs National Preserve, also on the western side of Atlanta, contains artifacts of the battle of Utoy Church.

One other site of note is Stone Mountain Park, east of Atlanta, the location of the largest bas-relief in the world, a 90 x 190-foot carving of Jefferson Davis, Robert E. Lee, and Stonewall Jackson.

FURTHER READING

Battles and Leaders of the Civil War, Vol. IV (reprint by the Archive Society, 1991)

Blount, Russell W., Jr., *The Battles of New Hope Church* (Pelican Publishing Company, Inc., 2010)

Blount, Russell W., Jr., *Clash at Kennesaw* (Pelican Publishing Company, Inc., 2012)

Boatner, Mark M., III, *The Civil War Dictionary* (Random House, 1959)

Cox, Jacob D., *Atlanta*, from the Campaigns of the Civil War series (original copyright by Charles Scribner's Sons, 1882, republished by Broadfoot Publishing Company, 1989)

Davis, William C. (ed.), *The Confederate General*, Vols 1–6 (National Historical Society, 1991)

Echoes of Glory: Illustrated Atlas of the Civil War (Time-Life Books, 1991)

Hess, Earl J., *Kennesaw Mountain: Sherman, Johnston, and the Atlanta Campaign* (The University of North Carolina Press, 2013)

Johnston, J. E., *Narrative of Military Operations* (D. Appleton and Company, 1874)

Key, William, *The Battle of Atlanta and the Georgia Campaign* (revised edition, Peachtree Publishers, 1981)

Lewis, Lloyd, *Sherman: Fighting Prophet*, Vols 1 & 2 (special edition by Easton Press, 1991)

Secrist, Philip L., *The Battle of Resaca* (Mercer University Press, 2010)

Sherman, William Tecumseh, *Memoirs of General William T. Sherman* (Literary Classics of the United States, Inc., 1990)

Symonds, Craig L., *A Battlefield Atlas of the Civil War* (The Nautical Aviation Publishing Company of America, 1983)

War of the Rebellion, Official Records of the Union and Confederate Armies, Series I, Vol. 38, Parts I–V (republished by the National Historical Society, 1971)

INDEX